MAMA knows BEST

THE REALITY OF PARENTAL RIGHTS

HANNAH SHIELDS

Copyright © 2019 by Hannah Shields. Book design copyright © 2019 Growing Healthy Homes LLC™. Cover design copyright © 2019 by Hannah Shields. Gentle Babies references and quotes used with permission from Debra Raybern. Gentle Babies © 2019 Debra Raybern. All rights reserved. No part of this book may be reproduced or transmitted in any form or by any means, electronic, mechanical, photocopying or recording without the express written permission of the author and publisher. Scripture references are from the King James Bible, which is public domain in the United States of America.

ISBN: 978-1-7338967-4-0
Printed in the United States of America
First printing.

Growing Healthy Homes LLC
5701 SE Adams
Bartlesville, OK 74006

To obtain additional copies of this book, please visit www.GrowingHealthyHomes.com.

Required disclaimer: The information given in this book is for educational purposes only and is not to be used for diagnosis, treatment or prescription for any disease. Though essential oils have been used for centuries with only beneficial results and the contributors have all experienced powerful benefits from their usage, the reader is advised to seek the advice of his or her chosen health professional before using essential oils. The content of this book does not necessarily reflect the views of Young Living Essential Oils, LC, Lehi, UT, (YL) and is produced by Independent Distributors. All trademarks are used by permission. The author, publisher, contributors and YL bear no responsibility for the use or misuse of any of these products. The decision to use or not to use any of this information is the sole responsibility of the reader. Also, any and all suggestions for essential oils apply only to YL.

For Samuel, Moses, and Zephaniah, my greatest blessings: I love you more than life itself. I will always stand up for you because you are worth fighting for.

Table of Contents

FORWARD 7
GRATITUDES 9
NOTE TO READER 10
PART I: Zephaniah 13
PART II: A Broken System and Commonly Held Beliefs 39
    Belief 1: "Hospitals Are Always a Safe Place With My Best Interest At Heart" 40
    Belief 2: "Doctors Always Know Best" 43
    Belief 3: "Doctors Will Not Test, Prescribe, or Treat Without a Good Reason" 47
    Belief 4: "My Doctor Will Fully Inform Me and I Have The Right To Choose" 53

PART III: A Better Mindset Towards Health and Home 59
    Mindset 1: Making Your Home the Safe Place To Be 60
    Mindset 2: Accessing The Expert Within You 68
    Mindset 3: Put The System To The Test 76
    Mindset 4: Maintain Your Rights 78

PART IV: Resources 85
    Appendix 1: Plants Are Your Friend 85
    Appendix 2: Wellness Routine 95
    Appendix 3: When to Seek Medical Attention 109

ABOUT THE AUTHOR 113

Forward

Hannah Shields is an author of Growing Healthy Homes, a publishing company owned by my husband Max and I. She is a talented photographer and graphic designer, and the work she has done for Growing Healthy Homes is very beneficial for Young Living™ distributors trying to share and build their Young Living business.

A few months ago, I read her testimony on Facebook about a hospital experience that led to her being turned into Child Protective Services. As I was reading her story, my blood started boiling! I immediately called her and asked her to please write a book about the incident. I also asked her to include the Young Living™ protocols that she and her family used before, during, and after her experience.

The resulting book is far greater than I could imagine! She has graduated from YL resources, to a book that will appeal to every parent in America that is concerned about their parental rights. Her research is impeccable! Her knowledge of using Young Living™ products is very valuable. I have assured her that publishing a book that holds knowledge about her use of YL products is also protected by freedom of the press in our Bill of Rights.

I am most proud of her for praying and asking the Lord Jesus for direction. I was unsure how she would respond to my request to publish her whole story, since "fear" is often the first response when facing agencies that have the power to force you to act in accordance with their belief system instead of your own instincts. She immediately told me that she was determined not to let fear stop her from doing what God wanted her to do.

She called me the next day and said that the Lord and her husband wanted her to publish her story so that other parents would not have to experience what she did. The medical system in America seemed to be established on the principle of the Hippocratic Oath, "first, do no harm." As you read Hannah's experience with her child in the hospital, you will be shocked at the harm the physicians and authorities did to her child and family.

No matter what your belief is about our Creator God or using Young Living™ products, every parent should be concerned about their parental rights in America. This book is one that every parent should read.

Hannah and I want you to know what your rights are before they disappear. I hope that you will join this fight to preserve parental rights. We have the right to say what we believe is right for our children until the state takes that right away from us. I pray and hope that day will never happen!

Thank you, Hannah, for your courage and passion for sharing the truth.

Karen Hopkins
Owner of Growing Healthy Homes Publishing
Young Living Royal Crown Diamond
Parent of 3 Children
Grandparent of 10 Children

Gratitudes

I want to say a heartfelt thank you to Karen Hopkins for reaching out to me and encouraging me to write this book. Thank you, Karen, for your prayers of protection and for helping me tell my story.

Thank you to my beautiful mom, Tracy, who shows me every day how to be a strong, resourceful woman who stands up for truth even when it is scary. You have always been my biggest fan and my greatest inspiration. I love you. Thank you for helping me find the right words for this book—it would not have been possible without your guidance and wisdom.

To my tribe, you know who you are. Thank you for being the freedom keepers and for always having my back. I will *always* have yours.

To my loving husband, Bart; you are the best decision I ever made. When I told God I would never marry a 'ginger,' he laughed and gave me you. He always knows *exactly* what I need. Thank you for loving me just the way I am and for always encouraging me to do my thing.

To Sarah, my amazing midwife, who guided me through a precarious situation with grace and ease. Thank you for always being your patient's best advocate, even when it isn't always easy or popular. I appreciate you!

Note to the Reader

The purpose of this book is to inform and motivate you by providing a quick but keen overview of our current medical system. This book is not meant to discourage you from seeking necessary medical care for yourself or your children, but to inspire you to get informed and know your rights before taking yourself or your child to the doctor or hospital.

This book is not all-inclusive and is not a substitute for your continuing education. This book is sold with the understanding that the publisher and the author are not intending to treat, diagnose, cure, or prescribe, but only to educate. If any such expert assistance is required, please seek the services of a competent professional.

The author has made every effort to make this book as complete and accurate as possible based on the information available at the time of publication. However, the accuracy of the content may change over time due to new studies, statistics, and laws. Therefore, this text should only be used as a general guide to understand your liberties and not be the ultimate source of information when seeking medical care.

This book is sold without warranties or guarantees of any kind. The publisher and the author shall have neither liability nor responsibility to any person or entity concerning any loss or damage caused or alleged to have been caused, directly or indirectly, by the information in this book.

PART I

Zephaniah

> "For God hath not given us the spirit of fear; but of power, and of love, and of a sound mind." —2 Timothy 1:7

It's time to speak up and tell my story.

It's time to be vulnerable and to break the silence of fear.

The fear of repercussions that would come from sharing this with anyone who may not know me personally or understand the nuances of what happened. The fear of offending someone who holds a different belief than I do. The fear of someone thinking I am ungrateful or unkind to those who care about me. The fear that I may receive negative feedback or retaliation.

Despite all those fears, I trust that speaking out and sharing my story may help a parent somewhere out there find the courage they need to stand up for themselves and their children.

I am writing this to you.

So here goes...*deep breath.*

> "What's the greater risk? Letting go of what people think—or letting go of how I feel, what I believe, and who I am?" —Brené Brown

ZEPHANIAH
(Whose name means, "The Lord has Protected.")

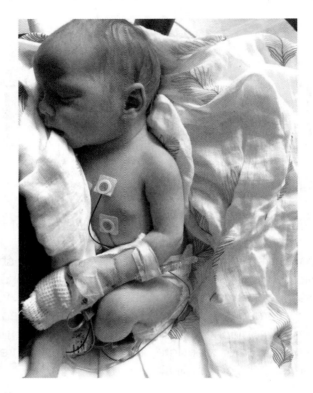

This is my sweet, little redheaded, baby boy, Zephaniah. He is only 22 days old in this picture, and as you can see, he is hooked up to a half a dozen cords and things that beep. I took this picture to remind myself to tell this story someday when the trauma had worn off.

I guess today is that day.

It all began in January 2019 when my husband, Bart, came home from an overnight work trip looking very ill. After suffering at home for a day, he decided to go to an urgent care clinic. While he was gone, I stayed home with our three boys. When Bart called me and told me he tested positive for Influenza A and was on his way to the hospital for fluids, I briefly panicked but then collected myself and kept my cool.

I had never dealt with the flu. A bad cold, yes! But nothing as severe as the flu, especially with a newborn in the house.

What I quickly discovered through an internet search—yes, I do that a lot—is that there's not much a physician can do for the flu. There is a costly prescription drug, Tamiflu™, that supposedly shortens the duration of the illness by one day if administered within 48 hours of onset of symptoms, but Tamiflu™ also comes with some pretty nasty side effects, and it can be especially dangerous for young children and infants.

The flu is a virus, which means it does not reproduce like bacteria and it cannot thrive and reproduce outside of a host body. It spreads by opening and releasing its genetic information into our cell's nucleus. The nucleus is where the cell's genetic information is stored. Using our DNA, the virus replicates, or copies itself, and takes over the functions of the cell. The copies of the virus go on to infect other cells, weakening the immune system.[1]

So, the best way to help the flu run its course quickly is to support the immune system so it can fight back quickly and efficiently.

---

1   "Overtreatment in the United States - NCBI." 6 Sep. 2017, https://www.ncbi.nlm.nih.gov/pmc/articles/PMC5587107/. Accessed 4 Sep. 2019.

> The National Center for Health Research state that the possible side effects of Tamiflu™ include: Nausea, Vomiting, Diarrhea, Stomach pains, Dizziness, Headaches, Seizures, Sudden confusion, Delirium, Hallucinations, Unusual behavior, and Self-injury.[2]

When Bart returned home after receiving IV fluids at the hospital, the baby started to seem a bit warm to the touch. He barely had a fever, just 2/10ths above normal. Healthy body temperature is considered 98.6°F, and Zephaniah's was just under 99°F. An actual fever is any temperature of 100.4°F or higher.

As a hyper-aware mama who notices every breath and eye twitch, I watched him like a hawk and checked his temperature about every 30-40 mins. After several checks that showed no rise in fever, I was still bothered by the fact that he might have the flu. So, I called the after-hours nurse at our pediatrician's office. I wanted to make sure I knew what to look for if he did have the flu. The after-hours nurse told me that a fever over 101°F is cause for concern, but to continue to watch him as I had been and call if anything changed. Thankfully, nothing did.

My motherly instincts told me that he was fine, and even though he may have been exposed to the flu, he was breastfed, very strong, and going to be ok. All my antibodies would help him push through it quickly. #breastmilkisamiracle

---

2   "To Tamiflu or Not to Tamiflu? | National Center for Health Research." http://www.center4research.org/tamiflu-not-tamiflu/. Accessed 4 Sep. 2019.

> According to the Center For Disease Control (CDC), "breast milk is the best source of nutrition for infants and provides protection from infections through antibodies and other immunological factors. Infants who are breastfed are less vulnerable to infections, including severe respiratory illnesses, than infants who are not breastfed. When a mother has the flu, her breast milk contains antibodies that can help protect her infant from the flu and breast milk remains the recommended source of nutrition for the infant, even while the mother is ill."[3]

The next morning, I had a previously scheduled, but totally unrelated, follow-up appointment for Zephaniah with the pediatrician. At the doctor's office, I mentioned that my husband was at home with the flu. Without even asking, the nurse swabbed the baby for the flu virus.

I had no idea what would follow.

The nurse rushed out, and a few minutes later, the pediatrician came in and informed me that Zephaniah had tested positive for Influenza A.

Shocker!

He told me that he had already called the on-call pediatrician at our local hospital emergency room and that I had two choices. I could leave immediately and take my baby to the hospital without any stops or detours along the way, or he would have an ambulance take him for me. He warned me that they knew we were coming one way or the other and that it would "not go well" if I did not show up.

---

3   "Influenza (Flu) | Breastfeeding | CDC." 4 Feb. 2019, https://www.cdc.gov/breastfeeding/breastfeeding-special-circumstances/maternal-or-infant-illnesses/influenza.html. Accessed 4 Sep. 2019.

Gut punch.

Holding back a flood of tears, I pulled myself together and asked a few shaky questions about why we needed to go to the hospital. He explained that the hospital would need to "monitor" Zephaniah because he was positive for the flu and under 30 days old, just in case he took a turn for the worse. He stated that newborns can go from appearing fine to death very quickly.

What?!

The thought of losing my brand-new baby boy terrified me. I promptly chose to take him myself and left immediately. I was sobbing all the way to the hospital. On the way, I called my husband, who was still at home sick as a dog, and told him that I was ordered to go to the hospital with our baby, or else.

I was an emotional wreck when I arrived at the emergency room. At that moment, I literally thought my baby was going to die if I didn't do exactly what I was told. I didn't know how to handle it. Something in my gut was telling me to run in the opposite direction, but I did what I was told because I was alone and afraid.

The emergency room staff quickly took us in, and I briefly met with a nurse and the emergency room physician. I was distraught, thinking about life and death for my baby. I was questioning my judgment, and thinking that if I hadn't shown up, someone would have come looking for me.

Meanwhile, the emergency room doctor acted as though he had never heard of me, why I was there, or what to do with my baby and me. It did not inspire any confidence.

Did I really need to be at the hospital?
Did the pediatrician mislead me?
Was my baby really in danger?
Could I leave?

With questions swirling around in my head, I resolved to stay, unsure I had all the facts. I explained to the ER physician that my baby had tested positive for Influenza A, and our pediatrician told me to come to the hospital emergency room immediately so he could be monitored.

Monitor, my ass!

What began was a cascade of events that all happened so fast it still feels like a complete blur.

They poked Zephaniah multiple times, trying to get blood from his tiny veins. They even jabbed a *massive* needle into his spinal column to collect fluid not once, but multiple times—*without my consent!*

Who do these people think they were?
Why weren't they consulting with me?
Why didn't they ask for my permission first?

The Mayo Clinic website states the risks of a lumbar puncture (spinal tap) to be: post-lumbar puncture headache resulting from spinal fluid leak, bleeding, back discomfort or pain, brainstem herniation, nausea, vomiting, swelling, nerve irritation resulting in tingling or numbness, and infection where the needle was inserted.[4]

---

4   "Lumbar puncture (spinal tap) - Mayo Clinic." 24 Apr. 2018, https://www.mayoclinic.org/tests-procedures/lumbar-puncture/about/pac-20394631. Accessed 4 Sep. 2019.

There was a frenzy of people coming and going with needles, catheters, x-ray machines; you name it. If they had it, they used it. After they had tried—*and failed*—to get everything they wanted from Zephaniah's tiny body, they dared to shove forms in my face demanding consent to the procedures after they had already performed them.

You've got to be kidding me!?

I had told them to stop repeatedly and told anyone who would listen that I was very uncomfortable with what they were doing and how they were ignoring me.

Now that they were done, they wanted consent?!

I demanded that someone tell me what they wanted to do, why they wanted to do it, and what the potential risks were *before* I would give my consent.

This was *my* child, and I wanted to be informed, but they had no interest in my rights as a parent. My children are my responsibility, but the hospital treated me like the enemy. They did everything they could to coerce me with fear tactics to comply or simply dismissed my wishes altogether. I wasn't the "expert."

I came to the hospital under the impression that they would "monitor" Zephaniah to make sure he didn't develop complications. They already had their diagnosis. It was the flu. Dad had, he had it, I probably had it…we knew the cause. But they treated him as if he was undiagnosed and potentially carried every possible illness known to humanity. In their words, "your baby is guilty until proven innocent."

Finally, after nearly 2 hours in the emergency room, the on-call pediatrician who knew we were coming to the hospital came in and spoke with me. She assured me that no more testing was needed, she was sorry for everything that had happened, and she was going to move us to a room for the night so we could rest and I could nurse my baby in privacy.

Seriously?! I had a sick husband at home trying to care for our two older boys, and they needed us to stay the whole night? My baby was showing no symptoms; no fever, no vomiting, no respiratory distress.

They had Zephaniah hooked up to a bunch of equipment, and to ease my anxiety, they promised to monitor him from the other room.

They insisted we stay, claiming the hospital was a safer place than home. Reeling from the whirlwind of events and still questioning my judgment, I decided to stay and follow orders.

After getting into our private room, nurses proceeded to come in about every 20 minutes for something. Rest and privacy was *not* the order of the day. Zephaniah had missed a few feedings, and his *"just in case"* IV contraption wouldn't allow him to lay comfortably to nurse. It continually set off the alarms every time he moved. Nurses would rush in to "flush" his IV—the method of clearing intravenous lines (IVs) to keep the tubes and entry area clean and sterile by sending cold and uncomfortable saline solution into his little arm. He was crying; I was crying. We were both a mess.

Lord, give me strength!

I looked down at my innocent little baby boy and kept saying, *"I'm so sorry, my sweet baby. I'm so sorry; please forgive me...."*

I called my poor husband four times an hour for moral support, but he couldn't be there with me in the hospital. I was all alone, exhausted, and traumatized—the perfect prey.

After surviving the night in our room with nurses coming in through what seemed like a revolving door, I discovered that the nurses were giving Zephaniah antibiotics in his IV without my knowledge or my consent!

I was still recovering from a cesarean section just three weeks prior, and I tried to limit the number of times I had to get up and down out of my hospital bed in the middle of the night. With the IV pole out-of-sight directly behind the head of my bed, I had no idea they were adding medications to his IV.

They were only supposed to be observing him, not treating him.

Zephaniah was not supposed to be receiving *any* medication without my permission. I made that clear multiple times. I was agreeable to having his IV in place for fluids or emergencies only, but I did not want him pumped full of unnecessary antibiotics unless his blood and urine cultures showed signs of bacterial infection. I thought there was an agreement between me, the nurses, and the doctor, but the nurse's flippant response of "it's doctor's orders!" proved otherwise.

Just like in the emergency room, my wishes were ignored entirely. To the staff, I was an annoying mother who asked too many questions and wanted to meddle in things I didn't understand.

At 9 am, almost 24 hours after we first arrived at the hospital, a new on-call pediatrician came to our room with nine other staff members to confront me about their need for yet *another* attempt to get spinal fluid from my baby's body.

Talk about intimidation!

The nurses could tell that I had reached my limit of unnecessary intervention for my baby, who was showing absolutely no signs of any illness. I felt like the staff came prepared for battle. Why else would ten people come to my room?

Another lumbar puncture—they already did three before I could even say no—was out of the question. The associated dangers of a spinal tap, coupled with non-stop visits from nurses exposing my son to dozens of illnesses from other patients was way too much of a gamble. The risk of life-threatening infections and further trauma for no credible reason was too much!

With lips shaking and knees knocking, I said, "No!"

According to the Centers for Disease Control (CDC), there are 1.7 million healthcare-associated infections every year. Suggesting that one of every 31 U.S. patients contracts at least one infection in association with his or her hospital care. The American Hospital Association Quality Center claims that two million patients in the U.S. get an infection in the hospital, and of those patients, about 90,000 of them die as a result of the infection.[5]

5   "Current HAI Progress Report | CDC." https://www.cdc.gov/hai/data/portal/progress-report.html. Accessed 4 Sep. 2019.

What happened next was unreal!

They told me that if I did not consent to another spinal tap, my baby would be forced to stay at the hospital for seven to ten days while they loaded him up with broad-spectrum antibiotics. Blood and urine cultures can take a few days to show exactly what kind of bacteria, if any, may be present.

There are other less invasive, diagnostic tools that can detect signs of bacterial infection almost instantly, but they weren't interested in using these. They insisted on treating Zephaniah with potentially dangerous, broad-spectrum antibiotics without knowing for sure if he even had a bacterial infection at all.[6]

The doctor went on to tell me that if I did not consent to the medicines, or if I decided to take my baby home, they would report me to Child Protective Services (CPS).

Wait! What happened to "just monitor him in a safe place" to watch and see if anything develops? And now if I don't do everything they say, they are going to report me to CPS!? It's my right and obligation as the mother of my child to ask questions and do what I think is best for him, and by doing so, I would be accused of neglect?!

In a culture where a woman can claim, "my body, my choice," it occurred to me that now that my baby was on the outside of my body, I had no choice in his medical care. Just a few weeks ago I could have made a completely different decision with the help of a doctor. It seemed like a double standard.

---

6   "Why Narrow-Spectrum Antibiotics Are Usually Better for ...." 14 Feb. 2018, https://www.uspharmacist.com/article/why-narrowspectrum-antibiotics-are-usually-better-for-pediatric-artis. Accessed 6 Sep. 2019.

I was not willing to jeopardize Zephaniah's gut health, immune system, or risk other possible health repercussions, including death, purely on their reasoning, "it's standard procedure" or "he's guilty until proven innocent."[7]

I had weighed the risks against the benefits for my child, and I did not feel the "benefits" justified putting his delicate little body through any more dangerous, invasive testing or treating. This was not my idea of monitoring.

Then things really ramped up.

The on-call pediatrician expressed concern about spinal meningitis or secondary bacterial infection. Zephaniah would have shown symptoms like a continuous fever, the lack of desire to eat, excessive sleepiness, bulging fontanelle (soft spot), vomiting, or rash, even others.[8] But no, none of this was happening to my perfect baby boy. Since the nurses were already giving him antibiotics behind my back and without my consent, any of the culture results they were hoping to find would have likely come back skewed. So, how would the new spinal tap serve him after he had already being treated with medication meant to kill the bacteria they were looking for? I may not be an expert, but this was not making sense.

Once I made my choice to decline another attempt for spinal fluid and ongoing antibiotics, the staff switched gears. They started to tell me that Zephaniah's lack of weight gain during our 24-hour hospital stay was a concern and that they were unable to get a consistent blood pressure reading.

---

7   "Antibiotic Use and Misuse in the Neonatal ... - NCBI - NIH." 29 Dec. 2011, https://www.ncbi.nlm.nih.gov/pmc/articles/PMC3285418/. Accessed 6 Sep. 2019.
8   "Signs and symptoms of meningitis in babies and ... - Meningitis Now." https://www.meningitisnow.org/meningitis-explained/signs-and-symptoms/signs-and-symptoms-babies-and-toddlers/. Accessed 4 Sep. 2019.

Where is this coming from?

After I urged them to retake his blood pressure with a different cuff, they discovered they had been using the wrong size cuff the whole time.

Seriously?!

After fixing that blunder, his blood pressure test results were excellent! Regarding his weight, I felt their desire for him gain half an ounce to an ounce of body weight during our short stay was preposterous given the fact that they barely left us alone long enough to nurse properly. Before our hospital stay, Zephaniah already gained more than a pound in the 21 days since his birth. Their desire to keep him for observation and supplement him with formula was utterly unfounded, and it seemed like a desperate ploy to put doubt in my mind and get me to stay.

Why were they so relentless?

Despite the barrage of nurse and doctor visits in our room continually jostling Zephaniah, he was eating a little bit, sleeping, peeing, pooping, and behaving like the healthy little guy that he is. Even the nurses kept commenting on how "not sick," he looked.

Hmmm. Why all this intervention for my baby who wasn't exhibiting any symptoms?

After the pediatrician and hospital staff left our room to regroup, it allowed me a few minutes to think. I broke down in tears. I didn't know what to do.

Should I stay and do what the doctor wanted or take my baby to someone else who would listen to me? Should I risk that the doctor would follow through with her threats?

All I wanted was to do was the right thing for my child.

I looked down at Zephaniah and asked him what he wanted. He looked up at me with his little trusting eyes, unable to tell me. I was his mama, and I knew it was my job to make that decision for him. I called my husband, and we talked about our options together. Given all the information we had at the time, we made a decision that we felt was the safest for Zephaniah.

We were leaving the hospital.

When I mustered up the courage to tell the doctor we were leaving, that's when things took a turn for the worst. The atmosphere completely shifted, and you could feel the tension in the air. It was hard enough to stand firm through the previous threats of my baby dying if I didn't do what they wanted, they now had a legal "risk management" official in my room (granted, they were covering their risk, not protecting Zephaniah). She approached me with guaranteed threats of calling CPS. I was told that it was "hospital policy," to notify CPS in the event a person leave Against Medical Advice (AMA), She also warned that our insurance company may not pay the $6,744.14 we already racked up in our one-day stay at the hospital if I left.

And to think, they wanted me to stay for a minimum of three days, but likely up to ten days. Talk about some serious hospital profits! Cha-ching!

After an hour of blasting me with every scare tactic available, the legal official left the room, and the pediatrician came in again with more nurses this time to coerce me to stay. She made it clear that Zephaniah was in no imminent danger if we were to leave, yet she seemed determined to find any possible reason for us to stay.

She also talked to my father-in-law, who was visiting us, taking advantage of his respected position as a physical therapist to convince me to stay. The hospital's frantic attempts to persuade me went on for nearly 6 hours. It was intense, uncomfortable, and meant to wear me down and cause me to comply, but my resolve was firm, and my mind was made up. Zephaniah was fine, and I wanted to get home and back to our routine.

I believed his Heavenly Father was protecting his little body from the flu symptoms and was giving me the strength I needed at that moment. The hospital and its overbearing staff destroyed my trust, and I no longer felt they had Zephaniah's best interest at heart. Their efforts to keep me there were motivated by desperation, fear, and arrogance, and were a complete affront to my right to leave. I signed the form releasing them from any legal ramifications of my decision, and we left with dozens of angry eyes watching, shocked to see us walk out.

After leaving the hospital, I decided to take Zephaniah to my parents' house nearby to avoid exposing him to Bart, who was still at home recovering. It also gave me some time to call my trusted midwife and explain what had happened. She quickly offered her services as my son's healthcare provider because she was a qualified, state-licensed midwife, and he was still within the first 6 weeks of life. I gladly agreed and made an appointment to have her come to my parents' home the next morning to do a follow-up check on Zephaniah. She also gave me the contact information of a pediatrician she trusted nearby, just in case I needed it for any reason before her visit.

At 10 pm later that same night, after vising my home and talking to my husband, the police came knocking on my parents' door with an after-hours CPS investigator.

The hospital had kept their word. CPS was on our doorstep.

They were insistent on seeing Zephaniah right then and would not wait until morning. I foolishly relented because I didn't want to take the chance of making them angry. With his mace open and hand poised, the officer and the female CPS investigator entered my parents' home.

Why were they here so late at night?
Were they here to take my baby?
Did I really have to let them in?
Inside, I was freaking out!

I did not know at the time that I did not have to open the door to CPS without a warrant. Instead, I stupidly allowed them to come into my parents' home, forfeiting my 4th amendment right to privacy. I allowed them to find any possible reason to take Zephaniah right then and there. I should have required them to get a judge-signed court order, which would have required them to come back the next day, giving me time to call an attorney and educate myself on my rights.

I have since learned they had no authority to be there, and that I could have said no.

Listen to the words of a former CPS investigator:
"I wish I could shout from the highest mountain to parents to vigilantly learn their rights! If they knew what

their legal rights were there would be significantly lower numbers of child removals. **Social workers, unlike policemen making an arrest, are not required to inform the parents of their legal rights.** *All we had to do to remove a child was to show up at the home and tell the parents we came to remove the kids. Often times we would take a police officer with us (never telling the parents he was there for MY protection, not to enforce an order or warrant). 99% of the time, we never had to get a warrant or court order to remove kids because the parents would be so intimidated by the officer that they would just hand their kids over and show up for court the next day. But if they had legally known their parental rights, they could simply have told me that I could not take the children unless I had a court order signed by the judge or had a warrant to remove the kids...the majority of times parents were just intimidated and gave consent for the whole process to begin; completely unknowing of what rights they just waived."*

During their visit, the after-hours CPS investigator desperately tried to persuade me to go back to the hospital. She promised that they would leave us alone, and the hospital would drop their claim of medical neglect if I would take Zephaniah back in for another spinal tap.

Grrrr...They already had his blood and urine, he had already received IV antibiotics, the doctor already said he wasn't in imminent danger, and he was completely symptom-free. What was it with their absolute obsession with my son's spinal fluid?

The whole interaction creeped me out. It felt like bribery. Like they were saying, "give us the spinal fluid, and we'll leave you alone."

The police officer and the CPS investigator stood there over my son's bassinet for the longest time, staring down at him. It was excruciating.

What were they looking for?
Did they even know what to look for?
Were they medically qualified to access my son's condition?

After describing what transpired at the hospital and why I felt the need to leave, I could tell that the police officer was anxious to leave. He made note several times that Zephaniah "looked fine" and that he understood my desire to protect my son from risky treatment without cause, but I knew he wasn't the decision-maker that night. He was there to protect the woman who was looking for a reason to take Zephaniah from me. I prayed hard and stayed quiet, but my heart was pounding. I was prepared to attack if she even hinted at reaching for my son. I have never been so afraid in my life! I had heard of medical kidnapping horror stories, but it was always someone else's story, not mine. Now they were here in my parent's home looking for any reason, like a sniffle or a hiccup, to take my baby from me. It was a real-life horror.

After taking a picture of Zephaniah, they finally decided to leave. I was shaking from the adrenaline but was so relieved. I firmly believe it was the power of prayer that protected Zephaniah from being taken from me. I did what I believed was the best for my son by leaving the hospital when I did, but my actions angered the hospital, and they answered back with retaliation.

I now had an open case with CPS. This was serious, and I knew their examination of my family was not over. They would be back.

Early the next morning, I began receiving phone calls from the hospital and our assigned CPS caseworker. I was scared to answer the phone; I didn't know what to say, and I was afraid I might say the wrong thing.

I spoke again with my midwife, and she offered to talk to our caseworker on our behalf. I was so grateful for her help. Knowing the terminology as a healthcare professional and being an advocate for my beliefs, she called our caseworker and explained the situation. Meanwhile, the hospital continued to call me every 20 minutes all day long.

After answering the first few phone calls, I decided to call an attorney. I felt like I was being attacked, and I needed a better understanding of my rights and how to handle the hospital's harassment. I called about a dozen offices to find someone who dealt with my type of case. I *finally* found someone. He answered on the first ring, and with grace and understanding, he talked me through everything I needed to know. He was a Godsend! He told me that if I went back to the hospital with an open CPS case, and the hospital staff determined that my baby was still in need of medical care—even if he may not be—the state would have the validation they needed to assume guardianship over Zephaniah, and potentially, my other children. They would have the right to make decisions for them as they saw fit.

No way! Was all this coercion to return the hospital their way of "legally kidnapping" my children?

The attorney was hinting towards that.

Not my kids!

I stood my ground, and we did not return to the hospital. Instead, our family endured multiple visits to our home, countless calls, emails and texts, check-ups, cops parked outside our house, the stress of the unknown, the constant fear of someone having the power to take our children, and more. For weeks, my husband and I felt like prisoners in our own home. We couldn't leave without thinking we were being watched. We jumped anxiously every time there was a knock at the door. We were nervous about taking our older sons to school, afraid they would be approached by strangers looking to take advantage of them without us present. We kept our house spotless, our refrigerator stuffed so full you could barely close the door, and the blinds tightly closed.

Even though we went through all of that, and it was terrifying, I know I made the right choice to leave the hospital. It is my job to make the best decisions for my children, and nothing, not even the threat of CPS, will ever cause me to shirk that responsibility.

I am very thankful for our midwife for being our advocate and for the CPS caseworker assigned to us, who was interested in the facts and ultimately respected my rights as a parent according to the law. I am thankful that the state closed our case quickly and recorded it as "unsubstantiated."

I am thankful for my husband, Bart and my amazing family who supported me and stood up for me when I needed to trust my instincts.

Most importantly, I am thankful for my healthy children, Samuel and Moses, and my baby boy, Zephaniah, who continues to thrive and grow every day with a smile on his face. He is perfect in every way.

> # IDAHO DEPARTMENT OF
> # HEALTH & WELFARE
>
> BRAD LITTLE - GOVERNOR
> DAVE JEPPESEN - DIRECTOR
>
> MIREN M. UNSWORTH - Administrator
> DIVISION OF FAMILY AND COMMUNITY SERVICES
> STACY WHITE - Program Manager
> Child Welfare
> 1250 Ironwood Drive, Suite 100
> Coeur d'Alene, ID 83814
> PHONE CDA (208) 769-1515 Lewiston (208) 799-4360
> FAX (208) 666-6744
>
> June 08, 2019
>
> Hannah SHIELDS
> ▬▬▬▬▬▬▬▬▬▬▬▬
>
> Dear Hannah SHIELDS:
>
> Idaho Statute 16.16.1605 requires any suspected child neglect, abuse, or abandonment to be reported within twenty-four (24) hours to law enforcement or the Department of Health and Welfare.
>
> On January 22, 2019, you were named in a referral of child neglect, abuse, or abandonment. We have completed our assessment in response to this referral and have concluded that the report was **unsubstantiated**.
>
> This notice reflects only the report dated above and the assessment completed as a result of the report. **It does not reflect the outcome of previous safety assessment(s) that may have been conducted as a result of any prior report(s).**
>
> Thank you for your cooperation in this assessment.
>
> Sincerely,
>
> *[signature]*
>
> ▬▬▬▬▬▬▬▬▬▬▬▬
>
> cc: File

Some information has been redacted to protect our privacy.

Thank you for allowing me to share my story with you. It is not meant to scare you, but to encourage you to be mindful. I want you to know your rights before you make a trip to the hospital or doctor's office.

You have the right to stand up for your health decisions with confidence, and you should never have to face what I went through. The only way to prevent medical tyranny is to build awareness, like I am, by sharing my story with you.

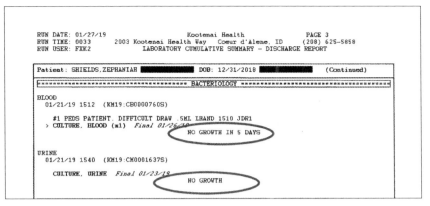

Some information has been redacted to protect our privacy.

Zephaniah—healthy and happy at 8 months old

People have asked me if my horrifying experience inside a broken system has caused me to be against hospital or doctors. The short answer is no. I respect medical professionals and the establishments they work in. However, I am pro-patient rights! I am a firm believer that once you have all the information, you are the best person to make decisions for your health and the health of your child.

I want to encourage you to do what you think is best for you and your family.

If you decide to go to a hospital or a doctor's office, go in with eyes wide open, educated, knowing your rights, how to keep them intact and be willing to listen to your instincts. They are a precious asset.

In the following pages of this book, I hope you will find encouragement, confidence, and the wisdom that you need to be the best decision-maker you can be.

PART II

A Broken System and Some Commonly Held Beliefs

> *"Failure is the system, and those of us who are not yet its victims are at high risk of being sucked into its turbines."* —Otis Webb Brawley, M.D., Chief Medical Officer of the American Cancer Society

We are continually bombarded by the media with a narrative that tries to convince us that our healthcare system is working beautifully, when in fact, it is failing miserably. The system has crumbled due to ignorance, intellectual laziness, greed, and regulatory organizations that have not done their job.

The first step in understanding your rights as a patient or parent is to have a clear understanding of the current medical landscape. In the pages of this book, I would like to ponder with you some of the most commonly held beliefs, or paradigms, that may or may not serve you best when making a decision about your health or the health of your children.

BELIEF 1

"Hospitals Are Always a Safe Place with My Best Interest At Heart."

"I would recommend to almost everyone that they try to stay out of the hospitals as much as possible. If you need to be in one, have someone with you, around the clock, as your advocate." —Andrea Stein, MD, Santa Monica, Ca.

Not that long ago, hospitals were considered a dangerous place to take your loved one for medical care. Founded and operated by religious organizations, our first hospitals relied heavily on volunteers and donations to provide charity care to the ailing poor. Armed with their motto, "no margin, no mission," they aimed to collect just enough money to cover the cost of their calling.[9] If people were affluent and could afford to pay for their medical care, they preferred to receive it from the safety of their home by their private physician who knew them personally.

It only takes a quick visit to a local hospital or a glance at a recent medical bill to realize that the medical system has transformed. The rooms are no longer filled with dangerous vagrants and inadequate equipment, and doctors are no longer making house calls. Our modern-day hospital has all the things that our antiquated hospitals did not: state-of-the-art equipment, esteemed specialists, and the financial means to serve the public in a much more organized way. With all the improvements we have made, are today's hospitals any safer than their predecessors?

---

9 "No Margin, No Mission: Flying Nuns and Sister Irene Kraus." 20 Mar. 2012, https://www.teletracking.com/resources/no-margin-no-mission-flying-nuns-and-sister-irene-kraus. Accessed 4 Sep. 2019.

After the introduction of medical insurance and Medicare in the 1920s, our humble hospital beginnings helping those who couldn't afford medical care morphed into a booming business. Replete with polished marble lobbies and grand pianos, social media managers, and bus-size billboards hawking their latest medical advancements, today's hospitals are trying to attract more paying customers. They are no longer operated by the church, but instead, greedy corporations with figureheads that recognize the potential revenue brought in by patients drawn to the newest testing equipment, specialty care units, and luxurious amenities. Today's hospitals are big business and big profits.

Even bigger profits are gained when hospitals build more Neonatal Intensive Care Units (NICUs). That might sound like a good thing, but studies have proven that hospitals tend to over-treat healthy babies to justify the expense of the NICU. At the cost of nearly $100,000 per bed per year, there is nothing more expensive to investors than an empty hospital bed.[10] A study from the New England Journal Of Medicine concluded that more NICUs and neonatologists in a region did not do anything to reduce the number of infant deaths.[11] It's clear to see the financial motivation behind more and more NICUs.

Today, pharmaceutical and insurance companies demand hospitals and physicians to deliver huge profits derived from the number of tests, treatments, and procedures they provide, not necessarily how well or how accurately they offer them.[12] Our medical institutions are hungrily eating

---

10 "Hospitals singing the "Empty Bed Blues" | Partners for Truth in ...." 26 Apr. 2017, http://www.truthinhealthcare.org/hospitals-singing-empty-bed-blues/. Accessed 6 Sep. 2019.
11 "The Relation between the Availability of Neonatal Intensive Care and ...." https://www.nejm.org/doi/full/10.1056/NEJMoa011921. Accessed 4 Sep. 2019.
12 "Types and Distribution of Payments From Industry to ...." 2 May. 2017, https://jamanetwork.com/journals/jama/fullarticle/2623606. Accessed 6 Sep. 2019.

up every opportunity to generate revenue to appease shareholders and affiliates.

When hospitals and the doctors who work there encourage any treatment, test, or procedure in response to malicious incentives, insane quotas, and precarious reimbursement systems, it can only leave us questioning our safety.[13]

Despite all its progress, does an institution with such a conflict of interest, genuinely have our best interests at heart?

---

13   "Dollars for Docs - ProPublica." https://projects.propublica.org/docdollars/. Accessed 6 Sep. 2019.

BELIEF 2

"Doctors Always Know Best."

"If people realized how little doctors knew, they'd be very scared and maybe take better care of themselves." —Lisa Sanders, MD, Internal Medicine Specialist and Associate Professor of Internal Medicine and Education at Yale School of Medicine

When we shirk our responsibility to act as the custodian of our health, we forfeit our rights to make informed choices, potentially putting ourselves in harm's way. Here are some things to consider before blindly surrendering your healthcare decisions to the medical system.

The Journal of the Association of American Medical Colleges agrees, "...if more citizens had more knowledge, and the will to act in certain areas, we would have healthier communities."[14]

Dating back to the early 1900s, autopsies were considered one of the most reliable, not to mention the oldest, way to learn anatomy and track medical failures. Autopsies consistently exposed alarming rates of diagnostic error, where patients often died of an undiagnosed or misdiagnosed cause. Despite modern inventions like antibiotics, pacemakers, transplants, and advanced medical imaging, the percentage of medical error has remained virtually unchanged since researchers began tracking results back in 1910.[15]

---

14   "Doctor Means Teacher : Academic Medicine - LWW Journals." https://journals.lww.com/academicmedicine/Fulltext/2001/07000/Doctor_Means_Teacher.13.aspx. Accessed 6 Sep. 2019.
15   Brownlee, Shannon. *Overtreated: Why Too Much Medicine Is Making Us Sicker and Poorer.* New York. Bloomsbury, 2007. Print.

Wait, what? Shouldn't our rate of accuracy be improving over the last century?

There is no doubt that modern medicine and its specialists are a marvel. The intricate knowledge of the human body coupled with recent medical advancements allowed specialized surgeons to take a small section of my husband's hamstring muscle and reconstruct his knees after tearing both ACLs.

It has also allowed me to bring my beautiful boys earth side three separate times through a small incision in my abdomen.

These are just two examples of how the practice of medicine has positively affected my family. I'm sure you, too, or someone you know, has benefited from advancements in medical science. Nevertheless, these fantastic feats continue to be overshadowed by the fact the United States ranks as number one in the world for medical error.[16]

Recent studies estimate medical mistakes may account for as many as 400,000 deaths annually, making medical error the third leading cause of death in our country.[17] What is even more shocking is that only 10 percent of medical error cases are reported each year—which means our medical system accounts for more deaths than heart disease, cancer, and auto accidents combined!

There were 36,510,207 hospital admissions in 2017, which means that one in every nine people admitted to the hospital were potential victims of medical system failure, resulting

---

16   "Your Health Care May Kill You: Medical Errors. - NCBI." https://www.ncbi.nlm.nih.gov/pubmed/28186008. Accessed 5 Sep. 2019.
17   "A New, Evidence-based Estimate of Patient Harms Associated ...." https://journals.lww.com/journalpatientsafety/Fulltext/2013/09000/A_New,_Evidence_based_Estimate_of_Patient_Harms.2.aspx. Accessed 6 Sep. 2019.

in pain, suffering, and even death.[18] According to the Institute of Medicine, "a hospital patient can expect, on average, to be subjected to more than one medication error each day."[19] Given these facts, it is foolish to overlook the evidence of medical error when making decisions for our health.

Through the internet, we have unlimited access to all of the same reliable sources of health information that our doctors do, *and we actually have time to read it*. Yet we are often ridiculed and feel intimidated by the "experts" when we try to discuss what we've learned.

For many, the doctor-patient relationship is sacred, with a level of trust comparable only to marriage. We trust doctors with our very lives, and in exchange, they give us, on average, 9 to 16 minutes of cursory examination.[20] This is not enough time to formulate a personalized care plan.

We are all different, but we accept a hurried, one-size-fits-all standard of care that restricts our doctor from doing what's best for us and puts us at the mercy of the system.

The word doctor is derived from the Latin, *docco*, which means to teach. However, this profit-driven, broken system robs the doctor of their duty to educate us.

Think about this. Customer service drives our current culture. We expect our local barista to recall the way we like our morning coffee. We get offended if our hairdresser doesn't remember how we want our hair styled. We demand excellence, personalized service from these providers; however, when it comes to our healthcare, we settle for

---

18   "Fast Facts on U.S. Hospitals, 2019 | AHA." https://www.aha.org/statistics/fast-facts-us-hospitals. Accessed 6 Sep. 2019.
19   "medication errors new.qxp - The National Academies Press." https://www.nap.edu/resource/11623/medicationerrorsnew.pdf. Accessed 6 Sep. 2019.
20   "Time physicians spent with patient U.S. 2018 | Statista." https://www.statista.com/statistics/250219/us-physicians-opinion-about-their-compensation/. Accessed 6 Sep. 2019.

second-rate attention from the people we put in charge of our health and the health of our children, especially in emergencies.

We receive an individualized bill, but we don't receive individualized consideration.

Our medical professionals are not all bad people purposefully subjecting us to potential harm. Most are good-hearted people who became physicians and nurses with a passion for helping others, but sadly, they are practicing in a perversely designed system that shields them from real evidence and facts. Despite our doctor's best intentions, the medical system in which they work is broken, and it claims too many lives for us to continue blindly putting our faith in the old saying, "the doctor always knows best." It is past time that we start educating ourselves and become active leaders in our own health.

In part three of this book, I have included some of the methods that I use to stay empowered and proactive in my family's health. Feel free to incorporate them into your daily routine as you see fit.

BELIEF 3

"Doctors Will Not Test, Prescribe, or Treat Without a Good Reason."

"Patients need to understand that more care is not better care, that doctors are not necessarily right, and that some doctors are not even truthful." — Otis Webb Brawley, M.D., How We Do Harm: A Doctor Breaks Ranks About Being Sick In America

We like to assume our doctors test, prescribe, or treat based on careful study, but in fact, they are manipulated by corrupt policymakers, deceived by skewed trials, urged by patient's requests, motivated by financial kickbacks, and frightened by malpractice suits.

In the following quote, Ben Goldacre, MD, author of *Bad Pharma: How Drug Companies Mislead Doctors and Harm Patients*, perfectly sums up how corrupt our healthcare system has become, and how difficult it is for our physician to do their job.

> "We like to imagine that medicine is based on evidence and the results of fair tests. In reality, those tests are often profoundly flawed. We like to imagine that doctors are familiar with the research literature about a drug, when, in reality, much of the research is hidden from them by the drug companies. We like to imagine that doctors are impartially educated, when, in reality, much of their education is funded by the pharmaceutical industry. We like to imagine that regulators let only effective drugs onto the market, when in reality they approve useless drugs, with data on side effects casually withheld from doctors and patients."[21]

---

21   Goldacre, Ben. *Bad Pharma: How Drug Companies Mislead Doctors and Harm Patients*. New York. Faber and Faber, Inc., 2012. Print.

When manufacturing companies can use flawed testing methods to exaggerate benefits and hide the truth about their products, there is no doubt that doctors will test, prescribe, or treat without reason. These are the very same corporations that subsidize our doctors and hospitals and create procedural standards of care. Many of these procedural standards are written to protect the corporation and its financial stake in the system, not the benefit of the patient subjected to them, creating an environment ripe for overtreatment.

Overtreatment in the United States is a real problem.

In a September 2017 peer-reviewed study, physicians from the American Medical Association responded to a survey about the extent of overtreatment. The survey asked specifically about the rate of unnecessary care, the most common reasons for overtreatment, and the relationship between profit and overtreatment. Out of the 70.1% who responded, physicians claimed that 20.6% of all medical care was unnecessary; including 22.0% of prescription medications, 24.9% of tests, and 11.1% of procedures. The most commonly cited reasons for overtreatment were:

1. fear of malpractice (84.7%)
2. patient pressure/request (59.0%)
3. difficulty accessing medical records (38.2%)

Physicians went on to say that they are more likely to perform unnecessary procedures when they profit from them—contributing to the nearly $300 billion of the $750 billion yearly excess healthcare spending in the U.S. That's an extreme amount of money in insurance premiums and tax-payer dollars, not to mention a lot of fear-induced stress and potential for harm for no logical, medical reason.

The same physicians offered possible solutions for curbing overtreatment. They suggested de-emphasizing fee-for-service compensation, better training on appropriateness criteria, providing easier access to outside health records, and having more accountability through practice guidelines.[22]

It is also vital to consider the role we, as patients, play in overtreatment. The United States is only one of two countries in the world that allow pharmaceutical companies to advertise directly to consumers.[23] With the permission of the Food and Drug Administration (FDA), pharmaceutical companies urge us to "ask your doctor if *(insert a drug name here)* is right for you!"

According to a 2011 study by C. Lee Ventola, "the average American television viewer watches as many as nine drug ads a day, totaling 16 hours per year, which far exceeds the amount of time the average individual spends with a primary care physician."[24] Disease-peddling pharmaceutical companies are encouraging patients to inquire and apply pressure on their doctors to prescribe medications that may be dangerous and ineffective. Doctors fall prey to this pressure because they are protective of their business and the compensation they receive. Meanwhile, drug companies are making $3.20 for every dollar they spend on consumer ads.[25] Don't be fooled by these multi-million-dollar marketing strategies.

---

22   "Overtreatment in the United States - NCBI." 6 Sep. 2017, https://www.ncbi.nlm.nih.gov/pmc/articles/PMC5587107/. Accessed 6 Sep. 2019.
23   "US doctor group calls for ban on drug advertising to ... - Reuters." 17 Nov. 2015, https://www.reuters.com/article/us-pharmaceuticals-advertising/u-s-doctor-group-calls-for-ban-on-drug-advertising-to-consumers-idUSKCN0T62WT20151117. Accessed 6 Sep. 2019.
24   "Direct-to-Consumer Pharmaceutical ...." https://www.ncbi.nlm.nih.gov/pmc/articles/PMC3278148/. Accessed 6 Sep. 2019.
25   Brownlee, Shannon. *Overtreated: Why Too Much Medicine Is Making Us Sicker and Poorer*. New York. Bloomsbury, 2007. Print.

It is a common misconception among patients that the FDA would never allow a doctor to prescribe a drug that wasn't intended to treat a patient safely. The FDA's job is to approve the indications of a drug—the symptoms that a medication manages. They also govern the accuracy of the label or packaging insert that includes how to take a medication for its indicated use. What the FDA does *not* do is regulate the practice of medicine.[26] Meaning, doctors may prescribe a medication that falls outside of its FDA approved use without any legal consequences.

Because similar symptoms can represent a myriad of different illnesses, and administering the wrong treatment could be detrimental, caution *must* be used when considering your options. It is your job to read *all* the packaging inserts, educate yourself, and consult with your physician on all your options before moving forward with any type of treatment.

This reminds me of a recently watched episode of the Netflix documentary, "Diagnosis," where a 6-year-old girl was having paralyzing seizures every few minutes. The seizures had gone on for months, and the doctors at the hospital were baffled in their efforts to find a cause. Her symptoms were presenting like a condition that only had one treatment option—a hemispherectomy—where they detach or remove one half of the brain to stop the seizures, a barbaric prospect that no parent should *ever* have to consider.

As a mother, I can't imagine how that poor mother felt, especially when her daughter was perfectly healthy just a few months prior. Through the course of the show, the physicians encouraged the mother repeatedly to move

---

26   "The Dividing Line Between the Role of the FDA and the ...." https://dash.harvard.edu/bitstream/handle/1/8846812/cberry.html?sequence=2. Accessed 6 Sep. 2019.

forward with the hemispherectomy, convinced this was the only way to "fix" her sweet little girl.

Knowing that her daughter would never be the same if she went through with it, the mother decided to follow her intuition and ask for another opinion. She just couldn't accept this as her daughter's only option. Through her perseverance and willingness to seek outside help, the mother found another medical team that was able to diagnose her daughter definitively. They determined that the little girl was suffering from an acute infection called Lyme Disease. She had many of the symptoms, but because they presented differently in her body, Lyme Disease was something that none of the other former physicians had even considered. Thankfully, the little girl received a much less invasive and far more humane treatment to stop her seizures, a much happier ending than what would have been had her mother not trusted her instincts and been rushed to decide without all the facts.

When we do not hold doctors and ourselves accountable, we are allowing a system that is legally shielded from the repercussions of overtreatment to make critical life decisions for us. Unfortunately, doctors may not always be right, and they may not always use a safer and more natural approach first. Sometimes they will order unnecessary tests and treatment because they resolve it is better to practice defensive medicine than to risk being confronted with a lawsuit that could increase their liability insurance premiums or challenge their ability to renew their medical license.

Regardless of your doctor's motives, you should always know all the risks and benefits of any treatment plan. You must be willing to question everything, even your medical professionals, and seek a second opinion when considering anything that could cause irreparable harm, even if it means being threatened or ridiculed. The time to discuss risks, benefits and any conflicts of interest is before you must make those kinds of decisions, not when it's too late.

"If I don't know my options, I don't have any." — Diana Korte

BELIEF 4

*"My Doctor Will Fully Inform Me, and
I Have The Right To Choose."*

"Unless we put medical freedom into the Constitution, the time will come when medicine will organize itself into an undercover dictatorship." — Benjamin Rush, a signer of the Declaration of Independence

I've heard thousands of stories just like mine from parents claiming their babies were subjected to tests and treatments without their consent, not realizing that when they entered the hospital, that act constituted consent to the hospital and their providers. Many faced contempt and threats when they questioned their doctor's authority to perform those tests and treatments.

I once believed that when I took my child to the hospital, I still had to give my permission before medication, testing, or procedures were given or preformed. This is not the case. Just being there gave them the right to do what they wanted.

It makes me angry to know that our fundamental human rights as parents and patients are being diminished, subverted, and altogether disregarded.

If there is only one thing that you take away from this book, I hope it is this:
> **Medical autonomy and informed consent is your right as a human being and as the guardian of your child. You alone are the best decision-maker when it comes to your health and the health of your child.**

> Patient autonomy: The right of patients to make decisions about their medical care without their health care provider trying to influence the decision. Patient autonomy does allow for health care providers to educate the patient but does not allow the health care provider to make the decision for the patient.[27]

According to the 14th amendment of the Constitution, recognizing a patient's autonomy is the cornerstone of modern health care in the United States.[28] However, as parents, we are repeatedly villainized for invoking our right to make those choices. The philosophy behind medical freedom is that every individual, even a child, is an independent human being with different physiology and a set of beliefs. Those beliefs are shaped by our genetics, our upbringing, our religion, our culture, our values, and our personal experiences. Because of individual distinctions, it is not likely a physician, by their own admission, will always *"know"* the correct course of care for each of their patients. When parents and family members are fully informed, they are the best at making decisions.

It is NOT the doctor's job to decide for you. It is their job to educate you on the risks and benefits BEFORE any test, treatment, or procedure is performed. You *can* say "No" if you don't want specific tests, drugs, or treatments.

---

27   "Definition of Patient autonomy - MedicineNet." https://www.medicinenet.com/script/main/art.asp?articlekey=13551. Accessed 11 Sep. 2019.
28   "fourteenth amendment - GovInfo." https://www.govinfo.gov/content/pkg/GPO-CONAN-2002/pdf/GPO-CONAN-2002-9-15.pdf. Accessed 6 Sep. 2019.

> Informed consent to medical treatment is fundamental in both ethics and law. Patients have the right to receive information and ask questions about recommended treatments so that they can make well-considered decisions about care. Successful communication in the patient-physician relationship fosters trust and supports shared decision making. —*Code of Medical Ethics, American Medical Association* [29]

It is against the law to treat a competent individual against their wishes. Doing so may be deemed as assault and battery.

The line between medical freedom and doing what is best for the patient often gets blurred, especially when children are concerned. In the patient advocacy book, *Critical Conditions: The Essential Hospital Guide to Get Your Loved One Out Alive*, Karen Blanchard, MD, states that:

> *"...every physician and nurse you will encounter at the hospital has sworn to uphold the Ethical Code. This code promises that they will do good, avoid harm, treat justly, and accept the patient's wishes as the ultimate authority...But hospitals today are institutions struggling to survive in an environment where the authority is in the hands of the insurance companies rather than patients and their families."*[30]

The law states that medical professionals MUST defer to the parents because a child is not able to decide for themselves.[31] More and more, doctors are disregarding parents' wishes and holding their intellectual superiority

---

29   "Code of Medical Ethics overview | American Medical Association." https://www.ama-assn.org/delivering-care/ethics/code-medical-ethics-overview. Accessed 11 Sep. 2019.
30   Ehrenclou, Martine, M.A. Critical Conditions: The Essential Hospital Guild to Get Your Loved One Out Alive. California. Lemon Grove Press, 2008. Print.
31   "Treatment decisions regarding infants, children and ... - NCBI." https://www.ncbi.nlm.nih.gov/pmc/articles/PMC2720471/. Accessed 6 Sep. 2019.

over the parent thinking they know best. Or worse, parents are being bullied, coerced, and pressured[32] away from their decisions with threats of being accused of medical neglect and risking doctors reporting them to Child Protective Services if they decline medical treatment.

All over the country, the threat of CPS is becoming the gold standard of scare tactics when a parent asserts their legal and moral right to choose. Weaponizing a publicly funded agency to force parents to accept medications, testing, vaccinations, or medical procedures, or even ask for a second opinion is criminal and should have no part in proper medical care. This wastes taxpayer dollars and prevents this public service from protecting children truly in need. It violates our constitutional rights and further degrades our trust in a provider that we expect to behave honestly and ethically on our behalf.

I am here to tell you, from one parent to another, that you CAN rely on your instincts to know what is best for your child. When you have the facts—the benefits weighed against the risks—you are the most qualified person to decide for them. Don't ever let anyone bully you or tell you otherwise.

Be strong. Stand up for your rights and the rights of your children and get informed! Don't be afraid of your doctor or CPS. You can stand firm in the face of intimidation by knowing your rights, and you can feel confident in your decision when you know all the facts.

---

32   American College of Obstetricians and Gynecologists. Informed consent. In: Ethics in obstetrics and gynecology. 2nd ed. Washington, DC: ACOG; 2004. p. 9–17.

PART III
A Better Mindset Towards Health and Home

> [*"Please live a healthy life—medicine is an imperfect science."* —Patch Adams, MD]

I learned a great deal through my experience with the hospital and CPS. Some things I definitely did not know. Some things I did know but didn't take seriously, thinking they would never happen to me. In the previous section, I covered some very hard-hitting beliefs that many of us, myself included, either consciously or unconsciously believed about our medical system.

After sharing my story and examining some commonly held beliefs together with you, I now want to share a few things that I have gleaned from this experience. I hope they will encourage you to have a more favorable mindset towards understanding how the human body works and the importance of living in wellness. I also want to give you some practical ways to start making your home the safest place to be.

MINDSET 1
Making Your Home the Safe Place To Be

"When a flower doesn't bloom, you fix the environment in which it grows, not the flower." — Alexander Den Heijer

The food we eat, the water we drink, the toxic chemicals we use, and the unnecessary stress we put on ourselves could be making us and our family sick. Many of these self-imposed environmental factors are rarely, if ever, considered by our doctors or us when looking for a root cause for illness. Simply put, the things that could land you or your child in the hospital could be easily found right in your cabinets or refrigerator. The best way to keep your family well, and out of the doctor's office and hospital, is to be intentional about making your home a safe place to be.

Eat Nutritiously
Be committed to providing your family with healthy, nutritious food. The old saying has merit, "an apple a day, keeps the doctor away." Just like an automobile engine takes the right type of fuel to run, our body operates on nutrient-dense foods to function correctly. You would NEVER put anything but gasoline in your car. If we put the wrong fuel in our "tank," by eating a poor diet, we suppress our immune system, which makes us a prime target for infection and disease.

"You are what you eat, so don't be fast, cheap, easy, or fake." — Unknown

Be intentional with your meals. Enjoy them at the table. Reduce the reasons that have you eating on the run and stay away from prepackaged foods and GMOs. Eat real food like organic fruits, vegetables, nuts, and seeds. Make healthy food accessible in your home and consider quality whole food supplements in your daily routine.

> *"Let food be thy medicine, and medicine be thy food." — Hippocrates*

Check out *Nutrition 101: Choose Life!, A Family's Nutrition and Health Program* by Debra Raybern, Laura Hopkins, Sera Johnson, and Karen Hopkins from Growing Healthy Homes. It is a biblically based and scientifically-sound nutrition program for the whole family that presents the major body systems, how they function, their prevalent health issues, and the benefits of eating good food. It's packed with hands-on activities, science and art projects, and nearly 80 family-friendly recipes.
www.growinghealthyhomes.com/nutrition-101-book

Drink Clean Water

Has it occurred to you today that you are thirsty?

By the time you experience the sensation of thirst, you are already dehydrated. The desire for water is your body calling for rehydration. Your body's need for water is so essential that you could only survive about three days without it. Nevertheless, many of us walk around in chronic dehydration, filling our bodies with coffee, tea, soda, or just about anything but the plain, clean water we need to stay healthy.

According to the Mayo Clinic, "every cell, tissue, and organ in your body needs water to work properly." Without water, you would be unable to effectively get rid of waste through your breath, urination, perspiration, or bowel movements. Imagine if you could never flush your toilet. Without enough water, your body is unable to flush toxins, leaving you susceptible to numerous diseases, at risk for becoming septic, or even death. Water regulates your temperature, lubricates your joints, reduces pain and swelling, and protects your sensitive tissues, like your brain.[33]

The adult human body is made up of 60 percent water. A child's body is made up of 65-75 percent water. Drinking clean, uncontaminated water that is free from toxic chemicals that will not interfere with your body's ability to function is kind of a big deal. Unless you have access to private well water, the water that flows from your faucets is probably not a good option for you and your family.

The Environmental Working Group (EWG) website provides a simple search tool that allows you to see the test results for your tap water. Your town's water utility company conducts the tests per state and federal environmental quality laws.[34]

When I checked my city's report, it showed some terrifying cancer-causing and immune-suppressing contaminants: arsenic, nitrate, radioactive radium and uranium, and Chromium hexavalent. Referred to as the 'Erin Brockovich' chemical, or chromium-6, Chromium hexavalent is a toxic odorless and tasteless metallic element that effects more than 200 million Americans across all 50 states. Chromium-6 has some debilitating health effects like cancer, liver damage, reproductive problems, and developmental harm, and presents more significant risks to infants and children.

The EWG examined data gathered by the federal Environmental Protection Agency (EPA) for a nationwide test of chromium-6 contamination in drinking water. EWG's

---

33   "Water: How much should you drink every day? - Mayo Clinic." 6 Sep. 2017, https://www.mayoclinic.org/healthy-lifestyle/nutrition-and-healthy-eating/in-depth/water/art-20044256. Accessed 12 Sep. 2019.
34   "EWG's National Tap Water Database - EWG ...." https://www.ewg.org/tapwater/. Accessed 12 Sep. 2019.

report found that if left untreated, chromium-6 in tap water will cause more than 12,000 new cases of cancer each year.[35]

I'll take a tall glass of water, hold the cancer, please!

Chances are your city water is a lot like mine, full of scary things that can hurt your body, which means it's time to choose a good quality water purifier that will provide your family with safe, clean drinking water right at home.

I love my Berkey water purifier. It's super easy to set up, fill, and use. It doesn't require any electricity, and it corrects the pH and filters out everything that my family doesn't need. Plus, it saves me a ton of money not having to buy plastic water bottles that only end up in the landfill.

To check the results of your tap water, please visit www.ewg.org/tapwater.

Kick The Chemicals To The Curb

One of the most unassuming but probably one of the worst contributors to an unsafe home environment are the products that we use on our bodies and to clean our home.

After the birth of my first son, Samuel, I really struggled with my health. I was depressed; my digestive system was always upset; I had headaches regularly; and practically lived on ibuprofen. I could scarcely drum up enough energy without the help of several cups of coffee. I wasn't even 30 years old, and I already felt like I had a laundry list of health complaints and vices that barely kept me going. When my husband and I decided we wanted another baby, I knew I had to clean up my body. I started eating better,

---

35   "'Erin Brockovich' Carcinogen in Tap Water of More than ... - EWG." 20 Sep. 2016, https://www.ewg.org/research/chromium-six-found-in-us-tap-water. Accessed 12 Sep. 2019.

taking supplements, exercising, drinking more water and less coffee, and reduced the number of over-the-counter medicines I was taking. I figured it would be just a short wait before we would be pregnant again and welcoming our second child.

Boy, was I wrong!

What I faced was five agonizing years of secondary infertility that left me on a hormonal roller coaster ride, wholly depressed, and coveting every else's baby. For years I watched my friends, sisters, cousins—basically, everyone else but me—get pregnant. Month after month, I would get my hopes crushed again. Another test. Another BIG. FAT. NEGATIVE. I had turned into a baby-obsessed, crazy person, shattered and bitter that my body wouldn't do what I wanted.

In 2014, my sister-in-law introduced to essential oils and toxin-free cleaning products from Young Living™, and they were the game-changer for my health and my fertility.

Like many of my friends and extended family, I never paid attention to the health-destroying products living under my sink and in my bathroom, things that were robbing me, and my family, of our good health.

How did I not know about these toxic chemicals hiding in plain sight? Wouldn't the manufacturer inform me that they were terrible for my health?

Before Young Living™, if my grocery store had a frou-frou smelling cleaning spray or laundry soap, I was all over it. Fields of Lavender and Lemon Verbena were my jam. Never mind that they were all lab-created, filled with parabens, phosphates, phthalates, dyes, sodium lauryl sulfate, glyphosate, and utterly lethal for my family. Every time I cleaned the house, I would create a haze of toxic chemical residue that would cause my family to cough, wheeze, sneeze, have headaches, and leave us feeling irritable and moody for days.

According to the EWG, the average adult uses nine personal care products each day, with at least 126 unique chemical ingredients that are known, or likely, human carcinogens. That's over one thousand chemicals, most of which we apply before breakfast.[36]

When we choose more trustworthy products that are free from harmful chemicals, we reduce our exposure to things that can cause devastating effects on our health, making our home a much safer place to be.

To learn more about Young Living™ and my favorite products that I use in my home, please see Appendix 2 in the back of this book.

Banish Toxic Stress

Did you know that 75 to 90 percent of all doctor and hospital visits are for stress-related ailments and complaints?[37] According to the American Psychological Association, chronic stress is linked to the six leading causes of death: heart disease, cancer, lung ailments, accidents, cirrhosis of the liver, and suicide.[38]

---

36 "Exposures add up – Survey results | Skin Deep® Cosmetics ...." https://www.ewg.org/skindeep/2004/06/15/exposures-add-up-survey-results/. Accessed 12 Sep. 2019.
37 "Three-Quarters of Your Doctor Bills Are Because of This ...." 22 May. 2013, https://www.huffingtonpost.com/joe-robinson/stress-and-health_b_3313606.html. Accessed 12 Sep. 2019.
38 "Understanding chronic stress - American Psychological ...." https://www.apa.org/helpcenter/understanding-chronic-stress. Accessed 12 Sep. 2019.

Have you ever watched the animated Disney movie, "Anastasia"? If you haven't, it's a cute flick loosely based on the Romanov family in Russia. If you have, then you might remember the little albino fruit bat, Bartok, who proclaimed, "Stress! It's a killer!"

Bartok was right. Stress *can* kill you.

Science says that chronic stress can affect your brain, suppress your thyroid, cause blood sugar imbalances, decreased bone density and muscle tissue, raise blood pressure, reduce your immunity, and impact your ability to heal. It can even alter your metabolism, resulting in digestive disorders and unruly metabolic processes. *Hello, muffin top!* If left unchecked, chronic stress can cause significant upheaval in the body, eventually manifesting itself as illness.[39]

These days it's hard not to get overwhelmed occasionally. Between juggling work, family, and other commitments, we can become too stressed out and busy. Children are particularly sensitive to this type of stress, and its disastrous effects. According to extensive research from The Center on the Developing Child at Harvard University, "the biology of stress now shows that healthy development can be derailed by excessive or prolonged activation of stress response systems in the body and brain. Such toxic stress can have damaging effects on learning, behavior, and health across [their] lifespan."[40]

---

39   "Life Event, Stress and Illness - NCBI." https://www.ncbi.nlm.nih.gov/pmc/articles/PMC3341916/. Accessed 12 Sep. 2019.
40   "Toxic Stress - Center on the Developing Child at Harvard ...." https://developingchild.harvard.edu/science/key-concepts/toxic-stress/. Accessed 12 Sep. 2019.

One simple but powerful way that you can create a healthy stress-free home environment is by shutting off the tv and video games. Making time for family discussions and engaging in uplifting games and activities can reduce toxic stress in a hurry. Another effective way to manage day-to-day stress is diffusing or applying essential oils. Essential oils have the unique ability to stimulate the limbic system of the brain. The limbic system is the command center for all the body's hormones and emotions and is accessible only through the sense of smell. Smelling essential oils are a safe and effortless way to create a healthy home environment that promotes relaxation and diminishes stress.[41]

Nutritious eating, drinking clean water, using non-toxic household products, and employing some natural stress reduction techniques are some of the fastest, most effective, and affordable ways that can make your home a safe place to be.

---

41 "Essential oils used in aromatherapy - ScienceDirect.com." https://www.sciencedirect.com/science/article/pii/S2221169115001033. Accessed 12 Sep. 2019.

MINDSET 2
Accessing The Expert Within You

"We look for medicine to be an orderly field of knowledge and procedure. But it is not. It is an imperfect science, an enterprise of constantly changing knowledge, uncertain information, fallible individuals, and at the same time, lives are on the line. There is science in what we do, yes, but also habit, intuition, and sometimes plain old guessing. The gap between what we know and what we aim for persists. And this gap complicates everything we do."—Atul Gawande, Complications: A Surgeon's Notes on an Imperfect Science

It's time to dig in and start understanding how the human body works and how to distinguish healthy immune responses from actual dangers signs. Most of all, it is imperative to build your confidence to the point that you can trust your instincts. Since medical professionals are admittedly using their intuition, we should be using ours.

Here are some of the basics that will help you to begin accessing the expert within you. Are you ready to start trusting your ability to be the best decision-maker you can be for your health and the health of your family?

Healthy Immune Responses
As parents, we are so used to our child's boundless energy, their eager appetite, and their grubby little face smiling back at us. When we see them not acting themselves, we jump into supermom/dad mode to ease their discomfort. It is troubling to see our child in distress, and we would do just about anything to help them feel better quickly.

Despite our best intentions, we are often trying to defeat healthy immune responses like fever, vomiting, and diarrhea. These symptoms are evidence of the immune system giving "the boot" to something that doesn't belong. None of these are fun to experience (or a delight to clean up after), but we need to be knowledgeable about the differences between healthy immune responses and actual dangers signs. We don't want to unintentionally stifle the body's ability to recover naturally and quickly, and in doing so, potentially prolong the illness or allow it to become dangerous.

A Quick Word On Fevers

Guess what? Fevers are the good guys!

Sadly, fevers are often misunderstood for what they really are: a healthy bodily function meant to jumpstart the immune system as a first-line offense against invaders. Instead, according to a pediatrics study, 89 percent of parents get scared and reach for an over-the-counter fever-reducer before their child's temperature reaches 102 degrees.[42]

Our "fever phobia" prevents our child's healthy immune response from doing its job to create an unfriendly climate for the offending organisms. When the body turns up the internal heat, the microbes cannot replicate, and they die off. By rushing to reduce a fever with medication, we could we be causing our child more suffering from the side effects of the medicine, which range from liver and renal failure to severe skin disorders (e.g., Stevens-Johnson syndrome) and gastrointestinal ulceration.[43] Worse, we could be preventing their little body from being able to efficiently fight off infection. This can lead to further

---

42   "Benefits of Having a Fever | Parents." https://www.parents.com/health/fever/fever-benefits/. Accessed 12 Sep. 2019.
43   "Acetaminophen - Live Science." 5 Oct. 2018, https://www.livescience.com/42785-acetaminophen.html. Accessed 12 Sep. 2019.

complications, expensive hospital visits, and the likelihood of undesirable treatment.

So, why do fevers get such a bad rap?

According to Dr. Ari Brown, a pediatrician, and spokesperson for the American Academy of Pediatrics (AAP), "Nothing bad is going to happen if you don't treat the fever."[44] Despite their benefits, fevers happen to be one of the most common reasons that a parent seeks medical attention for their child. We read information with scary words like seizures, brain damage, and death. No wonder we are scared, and our doctors are quick to suggest treatment.

The truth is, fevers are rarely, if ever, dangerous. Seattle Children's Research Hospital, one of the top 10 children hospitals in the country, states on their website that "fevers with infections don't cause brain damage. Only temperatures above 108° F (42° C) can cause brain damage. It's very rare for the body temperature to climb this high. It only happens if the air temperature is very high. An example is a child left in a closed car during hot weather."[45]

Pediatric health care providers have a responsibility to educate parents regarding fever and its essential role in illness; however, there seems to be a lot of confusion about elevated temperatures, even among the professionals.[46]
Fevers are not only harmless, but they are also helpful. Sometimes they may be uncomfortable, but they are serving a fundamental purpose. Before we rush to squash one, let's give it some time to do its job.

---

44   "Benefits of Having a Fever | Parents." https://www.parents.com/health/fever/fever-benefits/. Accessed 12 Sep. 2019.
45   "Fever - Myths Versus Facts - Seattle Children's." https://www.seattlechildrens.org/conditions/a-z/fever-myths-versus-facts/. Accessed 12 Sep. 2019.
46   "Fever Phobia: The Pediatrician's Contribution ... - Pediatrics." https://pediatrics.aappublications.org/content/90/6/851. Accessed 12 Sep. 2019.

Some tried and true ways to make your child more comfortable during a fever is by using cool cloths on the forehead and rubbing a drop or two of peppermint essential oil on the bottom of the feet. One of my favorite ways to safely support a healthy fever or anytime I want to boost the immune system is by having my kiddos soak in a warm detox bath.*

Detox Bath recipe can be found in Appendix 2 at the back of this book.

It is agonizing to watch our children work through these normal immune responses, but we must allow the body to do its job. The human body wants to be well. Everything within its design promotes homeostasis and balance. Such a simple thing, like not understanding the benefits of a fever, has caused more harm and heartache at the hospital than had the fever been left to run its course.

Danger Signs
Please refer to the list in Appendix 3 for appropriate signs to seek medical attention when your child is feeling sick.

Trusting Your Intuition

> *"A mother's intuition is worth more than a medical degree." — Dr. Susan Markel*

A hunch, a feeling in one's bones, a gut instinct, butterflies, an inkling, a sneaking suspicion—whatever you want to call it—you have it! It's called intuition. Everyone is born with a natural ability or power that makes it possible for them to know something without any proof or evidence. Some situations require us to rely heavily on our intuition, especially when parenting young children who are not able to communicate what they want or how they are feeling.

We all are born with some gut instincts, but it takes time and practice to get yourself to a place where you can trust your intuition.

Here are five simple ways that you can cultivate your intuition and boost your decision-making confidence:

Number 1: Get Your Guts in Good Order

"The road to health is paved with good intestines." — Sherry A. Rogers

As a parent, it's your responsibility to maintain a healthy microbiome. Over 95 percent of your emotional stability is in your digestive tract.[47] Science is now proving that your guts serve as your "second brain." Those feelings you are having in your belly are 100 million neurons working together to help you "feel" the right decision. That's more neurotransmitters than in your spinal cord or the peripheral nervous system combined![48]

You must have all your faculties in order when making important decisions about your child's health. Consuming nutritious food full of nutrients and fiber and taking a good-quality probiotic and digestive enzyme every day are straightforward ways to ensure your guts are in good order.

Your child depends on you!

---

47 "Nutritional psychiatry: Your brain on food - Harvard Health ...." 5 Apr. 2018, https://www.health.harvard.edu/blog/nutritional-psychiatry-your-brain-on-food-201511168626. Accessed 12 Sep. 2019.
48 "Think Twice: How the Gut's "Second Brain" Influences Mood ...." 12 Feb. 2010, https://www.scientificamerican.com/article/gut-second-brain/. Accessed 12 Sep. 2019.

Number 2: Listen to Your Body

"Go inside and listen to your body, because your body will never lie to you. Your mind will play tricks, but the way you feel in your heart, in your guts, is the truth."—Miguel Ruiz

Pay attention to your breathing, muscles, and heart rate to see how your body reacts and what that reaction tells you. These are some of the physical responses your body will show you to get you to listen up.

Think back to a time when you were scared for a good reason. How did your body feel? Was your heart pounding? Were your knees weak? Did your skin tighten? Commit those sensations to memory. Next time you experience those same sensations, you will trust that your body may know something that your logical brain might not yet comprehend. Get good at cataloging your body sensations. They will help you tune into your intuition faster each time.

Number 3: Align With Nature

"Our human bodies are miracles, not because they defy laws of nature, but precisely because they obey them."—Harold S. Kushner

This one is easy. Does your intuition align with nature?

If your hunch does not follow what we know about the human body and how it functions, then it may not be your intuition talking. Your gut instincts will never go against the laws of nature.

Number 4: Pray

> *"If prayer is you talking to God, then intuition is God talking to you."* —Dr. Wayne Dyer

The scriptures say in James chapter one verse five that "if any of you lacks wisdom, let him ask God, who gives generously to all without reproach, and it will be given him." I believe that whether it is what to say or what to do, our creator will give you the wisdom to make the right decision.

Number 5: Find A New Tribe

> *"The intuitive mind is a sacred gift, and the rational mind is a faithful servant. We have created a society that honors the servant and has forgotten the gift."* —Albert Einstein

We are surrounded by opinions and what we "should" do, especially regarding choices for our health. Just because someone may make a different decision than you would does not make your decision wrong. Don't allow another person to pressure you into a decision that you wouldn't have made without their influence.

Have the courage to do what is best for you.

When you embrace the whole idea of a healthy lifestyle, you will meet critics, and you will challenge the status quo. Ditch the old beliefs that no longer serve you and limit the influence of people who don't take health seriously and have shirked their responsibility.

These aren't your people. It's time to find a new tribe!

> *"The only real valuable thing is intuition."* —Albert Einstein

In conclusion, the more you use your intuition, the better you will be at it. Think of cultivating your intuition as a lifelong investment. Making better decisions will positively impact your entire life experience, not just the moments when making decisions regarding your child's health.

Treat it as a process. If using your intuition is new to you, practice these tips every day.

Practice makes perfect.

> *"When trusting your instincts, often you'll make the right choice, and at other times you won't. But if you keep at it, you'll learn to more accurately read your internal compass and come up with effective means to act on it. But if you don't empower yourself to do this, who will?" — Ron Ashkenas, Harvard Business Review*

MINDSET 3
Put The System To The Test

"The art of medicine consists in amusing the patient while nature cures the disease." — Voltaire

Sometimes, despite our best efforts to stay well, we must seek medical care, but before you or your child receives any test, treatment, or procedure, it is important to ask your doctor some fundamental questions first.

To recall the right questions to ask, just remember to use your **B.R.A.I.N.S.**

B – What are the **benefits**? *(Do they outweigh the risks?)*

R – What are the **risks**? *(Side effects or possibility of inaccurate results?)*

A – Are there simpler, safer **alternatives**? *(Diet, exercise, natural methods?)*

I – What does your **intuition** say? *(What feelings, images, or thoughts arise?)*

N - What if I do **nothing**? *(Will you get worse or better if you do nothing?)*

S - Can I **slow down** and give this some thought? *(Is it emergent?)*

If your doctor is not willing or able to answer these questions to your satisfaction, then you must seek out someone who is! It is essential to have a doctor who is an ally in your health decisions, who is willing to do their job to educate you on all your options, and who can provide quality care regardless of your preferences. Be an active listener and ask for clarification on things you may not immediately understand. Communicate what is important to you, take your time to decide, and ask for help. Make the system prove to you that their preferred course of action is the right one for you. The best choices are usually made through transparency, collaboration, and mutual respect. Don't just say "yes" because you are already there.

How Safe is Your Hospital?
Just like a restaurant, your hospital has a safety rating. It is a wise idea to check your local hospital's infection rates and safety data so you can be aware of any risks before going in.

Look up your hospital here:
https://www.hospitalsafetygrade.org

> *"If you want to know who controls you, look at who you are not allowed to criticize." — Voltaire*

MINDSET 4
Maintain Your Rights

"What the world really needs is courageous parenting from mothers and fathers who are not afraid to speak up and take a stand." — Larry R. Lawrence

It's time to take a stand and put yourself in a position of power before making any decisions regarding your child's medical care. You are the most vulnerable when you are under duress. These stressful moments could end up making you feel compelled to make a decision you wouldn't have otherwise made without someone pressuring you.

To make quality choices, you must gather all the facts, understand how the human body works, be willing to trust your intuition and be knowledgeable of your rights.

Your Rights When Seeking Medical Care:
- You have the right to have a patient advocate present with you at all times.
- You have the right to read all the product inserts from the manufacturer, not just the bulleted "facts sheet." *Bring a magnifying glass!*
- You have the right to say no to any test, treatment, or procedure, including antibiotics, vaccinations, supplements, any diagnostic test or procedure, or any other medications.*
- You have the right to choose your physician/provider.
- You have the right to leave.
- You have a right to seek a second opinion.

- You have the right to decide, free from force, fraud, deceit, duress, non-emergent time constraints, overreaching, or other ulterior forms of restraint or coercion. *(A consent form signed under duress is not valid.)*
- You have the right to contest any charges on your bill with your insurance company.
- You have the right to privacy and confidentiality with other patients, any medical caregiver, hospitals, laboratories, insurers, and even secretarial help and housekeepers that may have access to medical records.
- You have the right to receive quality medical care even if you do not have insurance or the ability to pay at the time of service.
- You have the right to open and honest communication.
- You have the right to informed consent (Including what the doctor is proposing to do, whether the doctor's proposal is a minor procedure or major surgery, the nature and purpose of the treatment, the intended effects versus possible side effects, the risks, and anticipated benefits involved, and all reasonable alternatives including risks and potential benefits).

*State laws may vary, but they should abide by the United States Constitution. Please check your state statutes.

> *"Knowledge is power. Information is liberating. Education is the premise of progress, in every society, in every family." — Kofi Annan*

How To Handle CPS

If CPS comes to your door, don't fret; here are ways to handle it with professionalism and within your constitutional rights.

1. **Take it seriously.** Even though CPS may be there for fictitious and ridiculous reasons, treat the situation seriously.
2. **Ask for details.** You are entitled to know what actions you are being accused of committing. Don't settle for "neglect" or "abuse" as an answer. Require them to elaborate. Ask for their name and the name of their supervisor and get a copy of their badge.
3. **Stop talking.** You shouldn't submit to a CPS interrogation before talking to your attorney. It is common for innocent parents who have nothing to hide to try to explain with lots of details so that a reasonable person can see that there's no real danger to their child; however, CPS agents are not reasonable. To them, the accusation IS the evidence against you. That caseworker is there to find evidence to support what they already believe to be true—that you abused or neglected your child. Saying nothing to them takes away their greatest weapon, which is to twist your words to fit their agenda.
4. **Find an attorney** who has experience fighting CPS as soon as you find out that your family is under investigation. Do not wait. Make sure they have expertise fighting CPS. Many attorneys will try to get you to follow along with CPS, and this could cost you your children.
5. **Be polite.** It's never a good idea to give CPS any reason to question you. If you must speak with CPS, this is an excellent opportunity to have your attorney or appointed advocate talk on your behalf.
6. **NEVER let them in your home.** Under no circumstances should you allow any government agent in your home unless he or she has a judge-signed court order. Ask to see the warrant or order

with your own eyes so you can validate its authenticity. You can say something like, "I understand your concerns, and I'm happy to cooperate with the law. May I see your search warrant please?" Make sure the warrant or court order has the magistrate's signature, shows the correct date, address, name, and pertinent information, and confirm that it also contains your state's official seal. Again, NEVER under any circumstances, let them in your home. If you allow a CPS investigator/social worker into your home, you have just waived your federally protected fourth amendment constitutional protection.

7. **Do not allow them to speak with your children** without you or your attorney present, and do not leave your children unattended in their presence. Don't even let them talk to or see your children through the door.

8. **Record everything.** Police officers and CPS agents are public servants, and they receive your tax dollars. You have the right to record them. If you are in a one-party state, you have the right to record conversations in private without permission from the other party. *(If you live in California, Connecticut, Florida, Hawaii, Illinois, Maryland, Massachusetts, Montana, New Hampshire, Pennsylvania, or Washington, please check your state laws regarding recorded conversations with government officials.)*

9. **Get family and friends involved in the fight.** Nothing is more off-putting to an investigator than having a massive network of people ready and willing to vouch for you. Ask friends and family to write letters on your behalf. If they decide to take your child(ren), give them a list of trusted family and friends, they can call for a placement. CPS investigators are required to consider such information, and it's much harder for

them to illegally kidnap your child without cause when they know a crowd is watching them.

10. **Never admit fault, guilt, or any wrongdoing.** Any admission could be grounds for them to take your child. CPS agents are not above lying to you or making things up to get you to admit fault. Don't make their investigation easy on them!

Remember: Medical autonomy and informed consent is your right as a human being and as the guardian of your child. You alone are the best decision-maker when it comes to your health and the health of your child.

PART IV

Resources

> "And God said, 'Behold, I have given you every plant yielding seed that is on the face of all the earth, and every tree with seed in its fruit. You shall have them for nourishment.'" —Genesis 1:29

APPENDIX 1
Plants Are Your Friend

Take a deep breath. Now exhale.

That action would not be possible without plants.

Think about this. Every breath we take requires us to draw oxygen into our lungs. When we exhale our lungs expel the byproduct, carbon dioxide. Plants absorb our carbon dioxide and turn it back into oxygen.

How cool is that?!

This symbiotic relationship between the human body and plants goes far beyond just the air we breathe. Plants provide us with clean water, warmth, fuel, and clothing. Plants even balance our ecosystem. But, most important, plants are our food and our medicine.

Without them, we would cease to exist.

Since the beginning of time, we have been intimately connected to the earth's provision. Plants can assist us physically, emotionally, and spiritually, and they continue to be at the center of research and discovery for the benefit of human health. I suspect your great-great-grandma readily relied on dried herbs, tinctures, and essential oils as medicine.

Plants were and continue to be easily accessible, and affordable options for common ailments. Today, millions of dollars are allocated to laboratories and universities all over the world that are searching for new therapeutic properties of plants. A quick Google Scholar internet search shows that their ability to assist the body in wellness is incredible and indisputable.

Despite all the hope and proof therapeutic plants continue to provide us, many parents are scared to use them in their homes and on their families. Instead, many look to a drug for relief before considering the plant that a drug is trying to mimic.

Why are we scared to listen to our creator and look to all of creation for a remedy? Why are we so willing to look to a drug company that spends more on advertising than they do on safety studies?

It takes an estimated 2.6 billion dollars to bring just one pharmaceutical drug to market, most of which goes towards advertising and regulatory agencies.[49] That's an insane amount of money spent on persuading the public towards a doctor's prescription pad, rather than educating

---

49   "Do Prescription Drugs Really Have to Be So ... - The Atlantic." 23 Mar. 2019, https://www.theatlantic.com/health/archive/2019/03/drug-prices-high-cost-research-and-development/585253/. Accessed 21 Sep. 2019.

us towards healthy, affordable, and useful plants, but you can't patent, trademark, or copyright nature, nor can you make a profit on well people that aren't popping high-priced pills.

Some may attribute drugs, and associated treatments for historically curing the incurable, but we must also consider how simple things like understanding basic human anatomy, handwashing, and flushing toilets have improved our mortality rates. Some drugs can serve a very pointed and timely purpose, and I am thankful they are there for us in real emergencies, but we shouldn't be so quick to use them when they are not necessary.

Here's the truth. We are not dying from a pharmaceutical drug deficiency. We are dying from a plant deficiency.

We have forsaken our trust in healing plants and put our faith in an industry intent on making us sicker and poorer. We should be embracing the abundant bounty of life-giving biochemical compounds found in plants, not using the wannabe knockoffs.

Every pharmaceutical drug out there has originated from a plant. In a lab, these plant compounds are isolated and studied until they become synthetically re-imagined into a patentable drug for the masses. The problem with these isolated and highly concentrated plant-mimicking compounds is that they can have serious health side effects.

Listen carefully to the next drug commercial that comes across your television. My dad always jokes, *"Ask your doctor if death is right for you!"* It's funny but real.

"Death is not an acceptable side effect for the attempted prevention of a curable disease." —Michelle Gaddie

Think of a plant and its chemical structure like an orchestra. There is nothing more beautiful to our ears than a symphony of instruments playing together harmoniously. Now, imagine listening to a concert where all you hear is a screeching violin. It's unbalanced, and it can wear on you after a while. When we use plants in their entirety, we benefit from all their advantages and built-in protective measures— no side effects like a screechy violin, just a perfectly balanced, therapeutic melody. *Ahhh.*

HERE'S AN EXAMPLE!
Cypress has 280 known chemical constituents.

If it is distilled for 20 hours, it will only release 20 constituents. If you distill it for 26 hours, it will produce none of the constituents. Most distilled cypress oil on the market for sale is distilled for 3.5 hours.

While you might get some of the smell at those lower distilling times, you won't receive the therapeutic benefits, or it may even be harmful. The correct length of time for distilling cypress is 24 hours to get all 280 beneficial constituents working together safely and effectively, like that full piece orchestra.[50]

You can probably tell by now that I LOVE plants, from their tips to their roots. Just like our bodies, they are miraculous. I could go on and on with stories about how plants have undeniably improved my life. I am so thankful that I grew up in a home that favored plants as medicine above all else, and they always bring me joy and comfort.

---

50   Raybern, Debra. Gentle Babies: Essential Oils and Natural Remedies for Pregnancy, Childbirth, Infants, and Young Children. Growing Health Homes. Oklahoma, 2019. Print.

One of my favorite ways to use plants in my home is through the use of essential oils. For over 20 years, I have used essential oils in some form or fashion but following my introduction to Young Living™ essential oils in 2014, my passion quickly grew. I began studying these little concentrated bottles of plant juice, and their benefits never cease to amaze me.

Have you ever cracked a twig or a flower stem or maybe scraped a tree and noticed a milky or clear fluid rise to the surface? That's the plant's essential oil. Essential oils are the protective aromatic oils that the plant produces to repair the damage, ward off pests, bacteria, and fungi, and ultimately protect the plant from environmental damage.

Essential oils can be cold-pressed, or steam distilled from flower petals, citrus peels, grasses, tree barks, roots, bark, and resins. Just like a plant's essential oil, our own body produces a similar substance, our blood, and lymph, full of red and white blood cells. Plant essential oils parallel our very own natural defense system. Imagine your body is in a war, and essential oils show up as allies with heavy artillery to help us battle against environmental toxins, fungus, bacteria, and viruses.

Can the body heal without essential oils? Yes! But essential oils help the body fight faster, harder, and longer.

> *"The natural healing force within each of us is the greatest force in getting well." — Hippocrates*

Unless you've been living under a rock, chances are you have heard of essential oils.

They are EVERYWHERE.

Every day a new company pops up with its own private labeled version. Everyone and their mother is hopping on the essential oil bandwagon. Why? Because they work! We are rediscovering what our ancestors already knew: essential oils from plants are powerful tools that can help us live longer, happier lives.

But before you rub peppermint oil on your child's feet for fever or diffuse eucalyptus to relieve their stuffy nose, there is something significant I want you to know. Not all essential oils are created equal.

An essential oil company's sourcing, science, and standards are critical criteria that you must consider before you get hypnotized by a pretty label. We are an investigative generation, and now more than ever, we care about where our food comes from, how it's grown, how it was packaged and delivered. We should hold our herbs and essential oils up to the same scrutiny.

Sourcing is everything.

You can't produce a quality essential oil full of therapeutic benefits from inferior plants and seeds. Safe and effective essential oils should be cultivated from thoroughly authenticated seeds and plants using agricultural practices that exceed federal organic certification requirements without using contaminated water, herbicides, and toxic chemicals. Plants must be harvested at their peak time using proper collection methods with precision before extracting, testing, and bottling their oils.

A lower price should never be a determining factor when deciding on a concentrated, powerful plant compound that you will use on the most precious people in your life. According to Jared Turner, Young Living™ Chief Operating

Officer, "it costs us around $12,000 per acre to weed our lavender fields by hand, using manual labor. Do you know how much "weeding" costs other companies? $60 per acre. Spraying cheap (and toxic) herbicides is faster and much cheaper." Don't "cheap out" on your family. You deserve the best!

> *"If you don't know your soil, you don't know your oil."* —D. Gary Young

Science allows us to advance in our knowledge and understanding of life-giving plants and avoid potential dangers. While a quality essential oil starts in the fields, its efficacy and safety are proven in independent and accredited state-of-the-art labs by highly skilled and trained scientists who specialize in advanced product testing. Testing should start at the farm and repeatedly continue throughout all the stages of production to ensure a safe and effective essential oil product.

Testing needs to include, but should not be limited to:

- Densitometry
- Viscometry
- Refractometry
- Olfactometry
- Polarimetry
- Inductively Coupled Plasma Mass Spectrometry (ICP-MS)
- Inductively Coupled Plasma-Atomic Optical Emission Spectrometry (ICP-OES)
- Gas Chromatography (GC)
- High-Performance Liquid Chromatography (HPLC)
- Fourier Transform Infrared Spectroscopy
- Automated Micro-Enumeration
- Accelerated Stability Testing

- Disintegration
- pH
- Microscopy
- Combustibility
- Flash Point
- Water Activity
- Gas Chromatography-Mass Spectrometry (GCMS)
- Chiral Chromatography
- Isotope Ratio Mass Spectrometry (IRMS)

The label on the bottle doesn't always tell the whole story of the essential oil contained inside. Many essential oil labels claim to be "100% Pure" or "Certified" but, unfortunately, most essential oils in the U.S. are cheap-to-produce synthetic, adulterated, illegally, or unethically sourced, full of pesticides, insecticides, and other toxic chemicals that can cause cancer and worse.

Don't be fooled by a label.

Use the same level of discernment for partnering with an essential oil company as you would choosing a mate. Have some standards. I know that might sound a little extreme, but essential oils influence emotions, hormones, and so much more.

You need to get to know the company first. Are they transparent? Are they practicing sustainability and protecting our environment? Are they using the best plants at the height of their therapeutic benefits? Are they testing and then testing some more? Are they using ethical business practices like paying their employees a fair wage? Are they keeping employees safe? Are they complying with government safety and compliance regulations? These are just a few standards that I like to investigate before I buy.

Make sure your essential oil company meets your criteria and don't settle.

For me, Young Living™ has been and will continue to be my best match. In all my years of using essential oils, I have yet to come across another company with more integrity, more dedication to quality, more transparency, more devotion to safety and efficacy, more humility and generosity, more desire to be the very best, or more heart than Young Living.™ When it comes to essential oils, they've got it covered, from seed to seal! (See www.seedtoseal.com.)

Young Living™ offers over 300 essential oils and hundreds of oil-infused products, and they are plant-based and 100% free from:

- Pesticides
- Herbicides
- Fungicides
- Formaldehyde
- Sodium Lauryl Sulfate
- Triclosan
- Parabens
- Phthalates
- Synthetic Fragrances and Perfumes
- Synthetic Dyes and Colorants
- Talc
- Bismuth
- Petrochemicals and Other Toxic chemicals
- Synthetic Preservatives
- Artificial Flavors
- Artificial Sweeteners
- GMOs

APPENDIX 2
Wellness Routine

"We are about lifestyle, about strengthening the body through nutrition and the power of essential oils. When we do this, the body will take care of itself. We are about self-improvement and living life to the fullest." — D. Gary Young

You don't have to be afraid. Remember, plants are your friend. And, you don't need to be an aromatherapist to begin using essential oils in your home. You can start today!

There are three simple ways to use essential oils: aromatically, topically, and internally as a dietary supplement. I'm going to cover the basics, some of my go-to oils, and how I use them when my family needs extra immune support.

Here are some of the most common ailments you can address at home with essential oils that may save you an unnecessary trip to the doctor or emergency room. This is not a comprehensive list, but it will give you a quick primer on how to start using essential oils when you are ready.

I will be recommending Young Living™ products because I have countless positive experiences and trust them explicitly for my family. Please note that I cannot guarantee the safety or similar results with any other brand.

WAYS TO USE ESSENTIAL OILS

Aromatically
By far, the easiest and quickest way to use essential oils is to smell them. You can open the bottle and take a deep breath or add a few drops to a cold-air diffuser.

Tests have shown essential oils reach the heart, liver, and thyroid in 3 seconds when inhaled. When you smell an essential oil, the olfactory quickly transports the microscopic molecules to the brain, where the limbic system resides. The limbic system is the command center for all your hormones and emotions. So, smelling essential oils can lift your mood, balance your hormones, boost your energy, and even open your airways for more clarity.

For a quick aromatic experience:
1. Place a couple of drops in the palm of your hand.
2. Rub your hands together.
3. Cup your hands over your nose and mouth and inhale deeply.

Topically
Topical application is a great way to support your skin and muscles because essential oils are fat-soluble and soak into the skin with ease. Some great ways to use essential oils topically are for muscle fatigue, inflammation, and skin irritation. Essential oils penetrate the epidermis and show up in the bloodstream within 26 seconds of application. They act fast!

Use fatty carrier oil like avocado oil, coconut oil, or V-6™ from Young Living™ to help smooth essential oils over larger areas. Using a carrier oil to dilute oils for infants and young children, or when trying an essential oil for the first time, is also recommended. Essential oils are very concentrated.

One drop contains approximately 40 million-trillion molecules, which is enough to cover every cell in your body 40,000 times.[51] So a little goes a long way!

Best application sites:

Bottoms of the feet: Your feet are thin-skinned, highly absorbent, but also very tough. The feet are a great place to apply mild and spicy oils without dilution.

Pulse points: Temples, neck, inner elbow, wrists, over the heart, groin, backs of knees, inner ankles, and feet.

On location: Oils can be applied right where they are needed, like a sore muscle, or achy joint. Oils can also be added to cleansers and moisturizers for bright, vibrant skin.

Internally (Dietary)

I love that Young Living™ has a line of Vitality™ oils that meet FDA-approved labeling requirements for their use as dietary supplements. You can add them to water or juice, place them in a veggie capsule, or use them to flavor your meals. In an average, healthy body, essential oils will typically stay in the digestive tract for 3-6 hours, allowing for maximum benefits. Digesting oils help with gastrointestinal health and supports major body systems, including cleaning up our lymphatic system.

Regardless of the method you choose, you will appreciate that an essential oil's benefits are typically noticed within 20 minutes. That means fast, effective relief for your family!

---

51 "THE BLOOD-BRAIN BARRIER - http://www." http://www.rnoel.50megs.com/pdf/theblood.htm. Accessed 26 Sep. 2019.

A quick precaution from *Gentle Babies* by Debra Raybern:
> *"Those who choose to vaccinate or use antibiotics with infant(s) and young child/children should consider taking a slower approach to essential oil usage until the child/children are a few days away from the vaccine or finished with antibiotic treatment. This is because pharmaceuticals may alter the body's immune system, which is what oils will strive to rebalance. This may initiate a response considered by those without an understanding of the chemistry of essential oils to be an adverse reaction to the oils. On the contrary, the oils are performing their natural function intended by God to help the body find a healthy balance."*

BE PROACTIVE!

Keep your family well by being proactive! When I know my family has been exposed to germs, we are traveling, or during the fall and winter, we bump up our proactive wellness measures.

- **Thieves® Essential Oil Blend:** Apply a drop on the bottoms of the feet in the morning and at night before bed. *For infants, dilute one drop of oil with 30 drops of carrier oil.*

- **Purification® and Raven™ Essential Oil Blends:** Alternate 5-7 drops in a diffuser to purify the air and support healthy respiration.

- **Thieves® Hand Sanitizer and Thieves® Spray:** Keep these accessible in your car, purse, backpacks, diaper bags, and gym bags for keeping hands clean on the go. *Think grocery store shopping cart handles, gym equipment, public restrooms, etc.*

- **Lavender Essential Oil:** Considered the Swiss Army Knife of essential oils, lavender can calm the body and provide quick relief for pain and discomfort. I diffuse lavender every night to help the whole family get deep regenerative and restorative sleep. A rested body is a healthy body.

- **Peace & Calming®, Stress Away™, and Valor® Essential Oil Blends:** Young Living™ has hundreds of essential oils and blends that can create the perfect atmosphere, but when emotions are running high, these are three of my favorite blends to apply and add to the diffuser. These blends create a sense of calming, grounding, and confidence in any situation.

- **NingXia Red®:** Fight free radicals and supercharge the immune system daily with 1-2 ounces of NingXia Red® superfood juice whole-body supplement. This sweet and tangy drink's formula includes wolfberry, which is revered for its health benefits, as well as plum, aronia, cherry, blueberry, and pomegranate juices and citrus essential oils.

  Children can also take 1/2-1 oz each day. Dilute in water as preferred. This is a tasty and effective way to balance blood sugar, provide nutrition and proper energy levels, and promote wellness. NingXia Red® is an excellent source of vitamins and minerals, antioxidants, and glutathione, which stimulates the immune system.

- **Super C™ Chewable:** Super C™ combines pure Orange essential oil with a proprietary blend of Camu Camu, acerola, cherry, and rose hips fruit powder to create a powerful immune-boosting supplement. Together, these premium ingredients deliver desirable polyphenols, carotenoids, and optimal amounts of vitamin C in a kid-friendly chewable tablet that contains 2,166% of the recommended intake. I typically give my children one per day, unless they are sick, then I bump it up to 3 per day.

- **ImmuPro™ Chewable:** A BIG thumbs up for this supplement. It's "mama's best friend" for helping everyone get a good night's sleep quickly while supporting the body's natural defenses with ingredients like wolfberry, a blend of reishi, maitake, and agaricus blazei mushroom powders, and orange essential oil. This supplement is also enhanced with melatonin, calcium, and zinc for extra support. No parent should be without this supplement! I give 1/2 of a tablet to my 5-year-old and 1/2-1 whole tablet to my 11-year-old.

- **Inner Defense™:** Create an unhealthy terrain for yeast, fungus, and bacteria with Inner Defense™. This supplement is a gel capsule. I typically take this myself, but if your child is old enough to swallow pills, then they can take this as well. Please read label instructions for proper dosage. For my little one who doesn't swallow pills easily, I will cut open the gel capsule and rub the contents on the bottoms of his feet.

- **Master Formula™ and KidScents® MightyVites™:** Everyone needs to give their body proper supplementation if they are not eating adequate fruits and veggies. I ensure my husband, and I get our daily vitamins and minerals with Master Formula™, and I give my children the whole-food chewable vitamin supplement, KidScents® MightyVites™.

- **Life 9™ and KidScents® MightyPro™:** Healthy gut flora is EVERYTHING. Good probiotics are vital for keeping harmful bacteria at bay and supporting good bacteria that will reinforce the immune system. I take a Life 9™ capsule before bed, and my kids love the KidScents® MightyPro™ quick dissolve packets any time of day. They taste like a "pixie stick" and can be mixed into cold food, drinks, or taken directly by mouth. You can sprinkle it into yogurt or a bowl of cut-up fruit. Free from sugars, artificial colors and sweeteners, and gluten, and packed full of 8 billion active cultures. These are a family favorite! My kids beg for them.

- **Essentialzyme-4™ and KidScents® MightyZyme™:** For the relief of occasional symptoms including fullness, pressure, bloating, gas, pain, and minor cramping that may occur after eating. Young Living™ offers five different digestive enzymes, but Essentialzyme-4™ is my personal favorite. It is a two-capsule supplement that is taken together and absorbs at various strategic locations within the gastrointestinal tract for optimal performance. To make digestive enzymes easy for kids to enjoy, Young Living™ formulated a chewable version, called KidScents® MightyZyme™ to be taken with or before meals. Digestive enzymes are beneficial for those who have food allergies, sensitive stomachs, get constipated, or have diarrhea or may struggle with other digestive discomforts after eating. I also highly recommend an excellent digestive enzyme for children that suffer from skin issues.

REACTIVE REMEDIES

Sometimes, despite our best efforts, the creeping crud works its way into our lives. Here are some of my personal essential oil remedies that I use in addition to my proactive oils and supplements to combat ailments in my home.

EARACHE
- 3 Drops Lavender Essential Oil
- 3 Drops Tea Tree Essential Oil
- 3 Drops Helichrysum Essential Oil
- 1 Drop Peppermint Essential Oil

Combine all the oils with 1/2 teaspoon of carrier oil and apply two drops of the mixture around the outer ear, on earlobes, down the neck, and two drops on the bottoms of the toes (the reflexology point for ears). You can also add a drop or two of the mixture to a cotton ball and place it at the opening of the ear canal to relieve discomfort. Please do not place oils directly into the ear canal.

Magic Salt Sock
After applying oils, you can combine it with a Salt Sock.

A Salt Sock is basically just a white cotton sock filled with Coarse Sea Salt that you heat up and place on the affected ear for relief. Salt retains heat and helps to create a shift in the pressure within the ear.

To make:
Use an all-white cotton sock (no color or synthetic fiber). Carefully pour the 1 - 1-1/2 cups of Coarse Sea Salt (I like pink Himalayan salt) into the sock and tie a knot (or double knot) in the end. It should be about the size of your hand. The safest way to heat a Salt Sock is in a clean skillet, over medium-low heat for about 4-6 minutes. Pick it up and shake it around and flip it every minute or so, so it will heat evenly. Heat until it is hot, but not burning to the touch. Cover the ear and the area behind the jawbone with the sock and relax for a while.

SORE THROAT AND COUGH

Diffuse or apply KidScents® Snifflease™ and use balm listed below.

DIY Cough and Sore Throat Balm
- 1/3 Cup Organic Unrefined Coconut Oil
- 2 Tbsp Organic Beeswax Pellets
- 20 Drops Eucalyptus radiata Essential Oil
- 10 Drops Melaleuca ericifolia Essential Oil
- 10 Drops Lemon Essential Oil
- 10 Drops Rosemary Essential Oil
- 10 Drops Copaiba Essential Oil
- 5 Drops Thyme Essential Oil

Melt the coconut oil and beeswax over a double boiler. Let cool for a few minutes, then add the essential oils. Whisk to combine. Pour into a 4-ounce glass container and place it in the fridge for about 5-10 minutes to harden.

For older children and adults apply to chest and neck as needed. For small children and infants, apply to the bottoms of the feet as required.

Try Thieves® Tea
- 1 Cup Hot Water
- 1 Drop of Thieves® Essential Oil
- 1 Drop of Lemon Essential Oil
- Milk and Honey to Taste

Add oils, honey, and milk to water and enjoy! It tastes like Chai Tea. Kids love this recipe too!

Sore Throat Quick Fix
- 1 Spoonful of Honey
- 1 Drop of Thieves® Essential Oil
- 1 Drop Copaiba Essential Oil

Or, bigger kids and adults can try the Thieves® Throat Lozenges and Thieves® Cough Drops!

FEVER
For babies:

1-2 Drops Lavender—Apply neat (undiluted) to the bottom of the feet.

1-2 Drops Lemon—Apply diluted 1:30 with a carrier oil, to the bottom of the feet and along the spine.

For children:

1 Drop Peppermint—Apply one drop to kids' feet and along the spine to bring a fever down to a comfortable level. Can be diluted 1:5 if needed.

1-2 Drops Lemon – Apply diluted 1:5 with a carrier oil, to the bottom of the feet and along the spine.

Detox Bath Soak Recipe
- 1 Cup Epsom Salt
- 1 Cup Baking Soda
- 3 drops Thieves® Essential Oil
- 3 drops Cedarwood Essential Oil
- 3 drops Frankincense Essential Oil
- 2 drops Lavender Essential Oil
- 2 drops Copaiba Essential Oil

Mix essential oils with Epsom salt and baking soda and add to the bathtub with the warmest water tolerable. Soak for 20-30 minutes.

If your child is less than 3 months old, with a temperature above 100.4°F (rectal, ear or forehead temperature), and accompanied by difficulty waking up to be fed, difficulty breathing, rash, vomiting, not urinating, abdominal pain, or inconsolable or non-stop crying, please seek medical attention. If your child is 3 months to 3 years old, with these symptoms along with a temperature of 102.2°F for more than 48 hours, please seek medical attention.

COUGH AND CONGESTION
For babies and children:
- 3 Drops KidScents® Snifflease™
- 2 Drops Lemon
- 2 Drops Tea Tree
- 3 Drops Pine
- 2 Drops Myrtle or Cedarwood

Combine essential oils with 1 ounce of carrier oil. Then apply 2-4 drops of the mixture to the upper back and the back of the neck.

Thieves®—Dilute 1:30 and apply on bottoms of feet.

For older children:
Use the above recipe with 1/2 ounce of carrier oil.

RC™ or Raven™—Diffuse as needed.

Breathe Again™ Roll On— Roll between shoulder blades and over the bridge of the nose, like a breathing strip.

Idaho Balsam Fir—Diffuse for 20 minutes every 6 hours.

Chest rub recipe:
- 1/8 Cup Organic Unrefined Coconut Oil
- 1/8 Cup Organic Shea Butter
- 1/8 Cup Organic Avocado
- 10-15 Drops KidScents® Snifflease™, Raven™ or RC™

In a high-speed mixer, mix carrier oils until it becomes a whipped cream consistency, then combine with essential oil of your preference.

RUNNY NOSES
Add Lemon and Lavender to nasal bone and under nostrils as needed. Dilute 1:5 for infants.

SINUS PRESSURE
Combine equal parts Lemon, Lavender, and Peppermint and diffuse or inhale as needed.

VOMITING AND DIARRHEA
DiGize™ or KidScents® Tummygize™—Apply 1 drop around the navel or bottoms of feet. Add 1 drop of DiGize™ Vitality™ to 6-8 ounces of water and drink.

Peppermint or Spearmint—Smell from bottle or diffuse.

AromaEase™—Smell from bottle or diffuse.

IRRITATED SKIN
Skin Assist Salve:
- 1/2 cup of coconut oil or avocado
- 1/2 cup of beeswax pellets
- 20 Drops Lavender
- 20 Drops Idaho Balsam Fir
- 20 Drops German Chamomile
- 20 Drops Frankincense
- 10 Drops Tea Tree
- 10 Drops Purification®

Melt the coconut oil and beeswax over a double boiler. Let cool for a few minutes, then add the essential oils. Whisk to combine. Pour into an 8-ounce glass container and place it in the fridge for about 5-10 minutes to harden.

Apply to skin as needed.

For more recommendations on how to use essential oils and natural remedies for pregnancy, childbirth, infants, and young children, I highly recommend the book, *Gentle Babies* from Debra Raybern at www.growinghealthyhomes.com

ORDER YOUNG LIVING PRODUCTS

1. Make a list of the products you would like to purchase.
2. Have a credit card or debit card or check handy.
3. Call Young Living™ at 1-800-371-3515 or go online to www.youngliving.com to place your order. You must have an Enroller/or Sponsor number. This is the who shared this book with you or who first introduced you to Young Living™ Essential Oils.
4. For online orders, first, select your country, and then click on Continue. Follow the screen prompts by entering your personal information and the enroller/sponsor number.
5. You may choose to become a general customer and pay retail or become an independent distributor buying at wholesale and saving 24 percent. There are no monthly obligations for purchasing or recruiting, and no yearly membership renewal as an independent distributor; this can simply be a wholesale account for your personal purchases. If you desire, you may initiate a home-based business, but it is never required.
6. If you select the "customer" option, make your purchase, and when the product arrives, enjoy!
7. If you select the Independent Distributor, choose your kit (I recommend the Premium Starter Kit. It contains most of the products I referred to in this book). Then, select Continue Shopping to order other products or complete the ordering process.

8. Be sure to write down your new Young Living™ account number, personal identification number, and password for future orders. Then, wait for your products to arrive and enjoy!

APPENDIX 3
When To Seek Medical Attention

Accidents can happen, and kids get sick.

While parents can handle things confidently at home most of the time, there are times when we must seek medical care. Please use the following list as your guide.

Remember to go in with eyes wide open, prepared, and knowing your rights. You are the best decision-maker for your child!

Visit the emergency room if your child has:
- Difficulty breathing
- Arterial Bleeding, characterized by spurt with each beat of the heart, bright red in color and usually severe and hard to control
- Bulging of the baby's fontanel (soft spot)
- Severe allergic reaction (shortness of breath, lip/oral swelling, throat swelling, persistent vomiting, altered mental status)
- High fever with headache and stiff neck and inability to touch chin to chest
- Suddenly hard to wake up, lethargy, or weakness
- Sudden loss of sight, speech or movement
- Broken bones
- Body part near an injured bone that is numb, tingling, weak, cold or pale
- Heavy bleeding or deep wound
- Dehydration, which includes dry lips. Dry mouth, and no urination for 6 hours
- Red streaks on the skin emanating from an infection point, possibly indicating blood poisoning

- Serious burn
- Coughing or throwing up blood
- A fast heartbeat that doesn't slow down
- Vomiting followed by dry mouth, not crying tears, no urination in more than eight hours or acting very sleepy/"out of it"
- Rectal temperature greater than 100.4 degrees Fahrenheit in children less than 2 months old
- Anything you can't quickly address and successfully resolve yourself; seek medical attention

About The Author

Hannah Shields lives with her husband and three rambunctious young boys in the beautiful area of Coeur d' Alene, Idaho. Hannah is determined and nearly obsessed with supporting parents and teaching them about their rights. She believes it is paramount to help parents know how to make their home the safest place for their families. In addition to being a Gold team leader and wellness educator with Young Living™, Hannah is also a private pilot, an award-winning graphic designer, and has a love for horses, plants, traveling, and making gourmet sushi.

Listen to Hannah's podcast, Speak Up, Mama™ to learn more about the parental rights movement and to get involved, at www.speakupmama.org.

To obtain additional copies and for more information on other books by Growing Healthy Homes, please visit our website at www.GrowingHealthyHomes.com

Nutrition 101: Choose Life!

Gentle Babies

Road to Wellness: Roadmap for a Lifestyle of Health